D1451776

Ethical Writings
of
Maimonides

The publication of this work has been aided by a grant from
The Andrew W. Mellon Foundation

A Publication of the
Institute for Philosophical Studies

Editorial Committee
Milton K. Munitz
Nicholas Rescher
Parviz Morewedge

Ethical Writings
of
Maimonides

by

RAYMOND L. WEISS
with
CHARLES E. BUTTERWORTH

New York: New York University Press
1975

Library of Congress Cataloging in Publication Data

Moses ben Maimon, 1135-1204
  Ethical writings of Maimonides.

  Includes bibliographical references.
  CONTENTS: Laws concerning character traits.—Eight chapters.—On the management of health.—Letter to Joseph. [etc.]
  1. Ethics, Jewish—Addresses, essays, lectures.
2. Messianic era (Judaism)—Addresses, essays, lectures.
I. Title.

BJ1287.M62E5   1975   296.3'85   74-18951
ISBN 0-8147-0984-2

Library of Congress Catalog Card Number: 74-18951
ISBN: 0-8147-0984-2

Manufactured in the United States of America

CONTENTS

FOREWORD

This book brings together in a single volume a broad range of works by Maimonides dealing with ethics. While not pretending to be exhaustive, it is both representative and comprehensive. There are complete translations of his two main ethical works, *Laws Concerning Character Traits* and *Eight Chapters.* These are supplemented by selections that throw light upon both the practical application and the theoretical foundations of his teachings. The sequence of the selections is from the most concrete elucidation of ethics in the Law Code to the theoretical principles in the *Guide of the Perplexed* and the *Logic.* The final section of the book encompasses his view of the messianic era.

All the works included (with the exception of the *Guide*) have been newly translated with a view to precision and readability. Almost all the translations of these works already available in English are inadequate because they either are not precise enough or are not based upon the best possible texts. In some instances, new texts have become available since the earlier translations were made. The long letter to Joseph has been translated into English for the first time.

Our procedure in the case of predominantly Arabic works that contain Hebrew expressions is to set apart the latter with italics. Except for the letter to Joseph, the translators are responsible for the division into paragraphs and for the punctuation in the Arabic selections.

We are grateful for the generous assistance given in various ways by a number of people: Rabbi Hillel Gamoran, Erica Aronson, Norman Golb, Ralph Lerner, Muhsin Mahdi, and Rabbi David Shapiro. We have reaped the benefit of the guidance of Leo Strauss, may his memory be a blessing, in his pioneering work in recovering Maimonides' teachings. We are much indebted to Erica Aronson for her perceptive suggestions on how to improve the English style of some of the translations. We also wish to acknowledge our gratitude to Shlomo Pines and the University of Chicago Press for permission to reprint selections from the *Guide of the Perplexed.* Finally, our thanks are due to Dawn Ross for her devoted labors in typing the manuscript, as well as to M. Tivol of the University of Maryland and the secretarial staff of the Philosophy Department at the University of Wisconsin-Milwaukee for their typing assistance.

NOTES ON THE TRANSLATIONS

Laws Concerning Character Traits and *Laws Concerning Repentance:*
Trans. by Raymond L. Weiss, based on the Bodleian manuscript containing Maimonides' autograph, ed. by Moses Hyamson, *Sefer ha-Mada'* (Jerusalem: Boys Town Press, 1962); supplemented by the Constantinople edition of 1509, ed. by S. Lieberman (Jerusalem: Mossad Harav Kook, 1964).

Eight Chapters:
Trans. by Charles E. Butterworth and Raymond L. Weiss, based on a Yemenite Judeo-Arabic manuscript dating from the period 1240-1340, ed. by Joseph Kafih, *Mishnah 'im Perush Rabbeinu Mosheh ben Maimon* (Jerusalem: Mossad Harav Kook, 1963-68); supplemented by M. Wolff, *Acht Capitel* (Leipzig: H. Hunger, 1863).

On the Management of Health:
Trans. by Charles E. Butterworth, based on the Arabic text ed. by Hermann Kroner, *Fī Tadbīr Aṣ-Ṣiḥḥat* (Leiden: Brill, 1925); supplemented by *Manuscript EMC 789* of the Jewish Theological Seminary of America, a Judeo-Arabic manuscript dating from the sixteenth century (cited in the notes as JTS); and by *Manuscrit Hébreu 1202* of the Bibliothèque Nationale, Paris, a Judeo-Arabic manuscript dating from 1466 (cited in the notes as BN).

Letter to Joseph:
Trans. by Charles E. Butterworth and Raymond L. Weiss, based on the critical Judeo-Arabic edition of David Baneth, *Iggrot ha-Rambam* (Jerusalem: Mekize Nirdamim, 1946).

Treatise on the Art of Logic:
Trans. by Charles E. Butterworth, based on Israel Efros' revised edition of the Judeo-Arabic text, "Maimonides' Arabic Treatise on Logic," in *Proceedings of the American Academy for Jewish Research,* XXXIV (1966); supplemented by Mubahat Türker, "Mūsā

ibn-i Meymūn'un al-Makālā fī Ṣinā'at al-Mantik," in *Ankara Ün-
iversitesi Dil ve Tarih-Coğrafya Fakültesi Dergisi*, XVIII (1960).

Pereq Ḥeleq:
    Trans. by Raymond L. Weiss, based on the Judeo-Arabic text in
    Joseph Kafih, *Mishnah 'im Perush Rabbeinu Mosheh ben Maimon*
    (Jerusalem: Mossad Harav Kook, 1963-68).

Laws of Kings and Their Wars:
    Trans. by Raymond L. Weiss, based on the Warsaw-Vilna edition;
    supplemented by the Rome edition of 1480, ed. by J. Maimon
    (Jerusalem: Mossad Harav Kook, 1954); and by the Venice
    edition of 1574, ed. by D. Aramah (Jerusalem: Alumot, 1965-67).

INTRODUCTION

BY RAYMOND L. WEISS

Maimonides (1135-1204) developed his great powers of con-
centration and wrote his monumental works in spite of the
severe hardships of the Exile and his own "poor original
temperament and weak natural build."[1] His birthplace of
Cordoba, Spain, was conquered in 1148 by religious zealots, the
Almohads, who forced non-Muslims to convert to Islam. Maimonides and his family managed to remain in Spain for some
time, after which they moved to Morocco, and finally settled in
Egypt, which was beyond the hegemony of the Almohads. In
Egypt he continued his work on the Law and philosophy, while
being supported by his younger brother, a merchant. His
brother died during a voyage on the Indian ocean and Maimonides, who had helped to rear him and was deeply attached
to him, suffered greatly as a result. Eight years later, he says in a
letter that he was still in mourning, bereft of his only delight,
and living in grief in an alien land. After his brother's death, he
turned to medicine to earn a livelihood for the whole family,
and he eventually became a physician to the sultan's palace in
Cairo. This position had political significance, for it gave him
access to the vizier and other Muslim leaders when Jews were in
a highly vulnerable position. Maimonides himself was exposed
to peril because of the unorthodox character of his thought. At
one point he was denounced to the authorities by a Muslim for
allegedly teaching pernicious doctrines in the *Guide of the
Perplexed,* but nothing came of the accusation.

Whatever danger he faced as a heterodox thinker and an
alien living under Muslim rule, Maimonides was also able to
reap the advantages of living in a Muslim world that had
recovered the Aristotelian sciences. His intellectual kinship

1

with the Muslim philosophers transcended the rigid bounda-
ries set by religion. His agreement with them can be seen in a
common opposition to the Mutakallimūn, who used reason in a
non-philosophic manner to defend the tenets of revealed
religion. In *Eight Chapters* Maimonides opposes the contention
of the Mutakallimūn that there are "rational laws" for governing human life. Maimonides' denial of the existence of "rational
laws" represents a different stream of Aristotelianism from the
one that has nourished the West. In the Christian West, the
analogue to "rational law" is the Thomistic teaching of natural
law. There is accordingly an opposition between the Maimoni-
dean denial of "rational law" and the Thomistic affirmation of
natural law. I shall return to Maimonides' position later and
simply note here one implication which tends to justify the
need for the Law. If there are no "rational laws" for governing
human life, the particular Law of a particular nation becomes
all the more important.

The bulk of Maimonides' work is concerned with Jewish law.
Even the *Guide of the Perplexed,* with its extensive philosophic
speculation, aims at clarifying and defending the foundations
of the Law. His first work on the Law was a commentary on a
rabbinic law code, the *Mishnah.* His most important legal work
is the massive *Mishneh Torah* (or Code), in which the entire
corpus of Jewish law is codified. His only philosophic work per
se is the short *Treatise on the Art of Logic,* which does not
presuppose the validity of the Law.

Maimonides wrote no separate ethical treatises. His main
ethical works, *Laws Concerning Character Traits* and *Eight Chapters,* are part of much larger works on the Law, the *Mishneh
Torah* and the *Commentary on the Mishnah,* respectively. He deals
with ethics in a legal, or political, context. Since the Law is a
source of commands, it admirably suits the practical purpose of
ethics. In agreement with Aristotle and the Muslim philosophers, Maimonides classifies ethics as part of practical philosophy or political science. He could draw upon classical
philosophy for interpreting the Law because the Law governs
every aspect of human life and therefore meets the requirement of classical philosophy that law be comprehensive in
character. The Jewish tradition takes for granted what is taught

by classical philosophy, namely, that moral education must take place within a broader legal, or political, context.

The biblical-rabbinic tradition, however, does not distinguish ethics as such. It does not differentiate between, say, moral and ritual laws. To clearly delimit the sphere of ethics, Maimonides has recourse to the Aristotelian teaching according to which "ethics" refers to character traits. He demarcates this subject in the Code by gathering together the relevant laws in the section called *Hilkhot De'ot,* or *Laws Concerning Character Traits.* Maimonides was the first Jewish thinker to give special and explicit attention to the shaping of character in a codification of the Law.

In *Eight Chapters* he bases this conception of "ethics" as character traits on the nature of the human soul. Character traits or moral habits are found in the appetitive part of the soul, which contains the passions. Although a moral education requires that correct opinions be taught and that actions preparatory to virtue be performed, the goal is the formation of the right character traits in the soul's appetitive part. Ethics, then, is primarily concerned not with opinions, which are in the rational part of the soul, nor even with human actions, but rather with the moral virtues, which are noble character traits. They form the foundation within the soul for performing the right actions.

This conception of ethics establishes a connection between moral virtue and the domain of politics: the well-being of the community requires that its members have good moral habits. Maimonides emphasizes this aspect of ethics to such an extent that he says all the moral virtues are instrumental to the well-being of other people (*Guide,* III 54). The legitimate wish of people to be treated with decency is violated when the training necessary for acquiring moral virtue is neglected. One basis of the need for moral virtue, then, is man's political nature, his need to live with other human beings.

Man's political nature is based upon the nature of the human body. Man must live in society in order to fulfill the complex needs of the human body for food, clothing, shelter, etc. Maimonides comes close to viewing man as a social rather than a political animal, that is, one whose nature is characterized by

the need to live in society, as distinct from a polity. Man is
nevertheless a political animal because society must be ordered
through laws defined and promulgated through a recognized
political authority. Otherwise there would be chaos, or as one
medieval commentary on the *Guide* puts it, men would behave
like the beasts of the field.[2]

Maimonides does not contend that men are naturally vicious,
but that the natural temperaments of human beings vary
greatly. Some people for instance are by nature inclined to be
very compassionate, while others are naturally inclined to be
cruel. Antagonism and even warfare would result if the
"natural diversity" among men were not muted by a "conventional accord."[3] Nature in a sense drives men apart, but it
also compels them to live together. They therefore need a
common code of conduct to make anything resembling a
society possible. The mean is a standard that does not make
excessive demands upon the tendency of men to follow their
natural inclinations. It is a kind of compromise for the sake of
establishing a semblance of unity among people with extraordinarily different natural dispositions.

The well-being of society is not the only purpose of morality.
Moral virtue also produces serenity within the individual himself; a strict moral regimen is needed to quiet the disturbances
of the body's impulses. Equanimity is not an end in itself, but a
means for attaining the contemplative life. Put into a more
contemporary idiom, the most important human freedom is
that of the intellect to do its work well, and freedom in this
sense requires moral virtue to govern the passions. Thus, in
addition to man's political nature, ethics is grounded upon
man's rational nature. The proper standard, from this viewpoint too, is the mean, which keeps the body's impulses in
balance or harmony. It is remarkable that both man's rational
and political nature call for a mean in ethics. The basis of the
need for a mean in both instances lies in the nature of the
human body, understood from different points of view.

In spite of this agreement concerning morality, there is a
certain tension, not to say opposition, between man's political
nature and the contemplative life. The latter is essentially
solitary; there are no actions or moral habits involved in
contemplation (*Guide*, III 27). Or we could say that man's

political nature requires speech addressed to others, whereas the proper activity of the contemplative life, to form intelligibles, is "inner speech" (cf. *Logic*, XIV). Nevertheless, man's political and rational nature cannot be divorced from each other; the wise man is not a disembodied intellect. Because of his political nature, he is a member of a particular community and therefore has to follow the code of conduct governing that community.

Laws Concerning Character Traits (Hilkhot De'ot)

The laws in the *Mishneh Torah* "settle" the mind of man (*meyashvin da'ato shel 'adam*) and bring about the "settlement" or stability of this world (*yishuv ha-'olam hazeh*).[4] *H. De'ot*, which contains the ethics of the Code, aims at both tranquillity of mind and the well-being of society. It encompasses the moral requirements of both the sage and the community.

The overall movement of *H. De'ot* is from the individual's well-being to that of society. The first four chapters set forth primarily the morality of the wise man, who follows the middle way to attain his own perfection (I 4). Chapter Five, directed by and large to the disciple of the wise men (*talmid ha-ḥakhamim*), is concerned with actions in contradistinction to character traits proper and therefore describes the disciple's conduct with other people. It prescribes the business conduct of the Jewish sage, his sexual practice, his manners at the table, in walking, etc. The commandments in Chapters Six and Seven, which complete the work, are intended specifically for the people as a whole. The first commandment in this subsection is to imitate the conduct of the sages and their disciples (VI 2). It is followed by commandments regulating man's conduct with his fellow man, beginning with the commandment to love your neighbor as yourself, which is explicitly directed to "every man." It is striking that ten of the eleven commandments in this work are in the last two chapters, and quotations from the Jewish tradition abound in the last three. The regulation of conduct in society is clearly rooted in the Jewish tradition.

The first commandment in *H. De'ot*, to imitate God's ways, is interpreted as requiring adherence to the mean, which is the

standard followed by the wise men. Through this commandment, the morality of the sage is enjoined not simply upon the
limited number of men who are wise, but upon everyone. Since
the wise men and their disciples are the model for the whole
community, the laws prescribing their conduct are applicable to
all people. The ethics of the Code aims at the moral perfection
of every man, irrespective of whether everyone can be expected
to achieve so lofty a goal. In fact, the presumption is that most
people will not acquire all the character traits of a wise man
(V 1).

The two primary goals of the Code, personal serenity and
communal well-being, govern the brief definitions of the moral
qualities lying in the mean (I 4). The middle way in anger, for
instance, simultaneously curbs anger for the sake of the individual's own tranquillity and requires anger when necessary for
the correction of other people: the middle way calls for anger
to prevent a serious misdeed from recurring in the future.
Bodily desire is confined to the body's needs, a limitation that
eliminates excessive stimulation or excitement and helps to
"settle" the mind. This restriction serves the community by
dampening the acquisitive passion, which Maimonides regards
as the root of most of the evils in cities.[5] The middle way
includes a consistently joyful disposition which, besides its
benefit for human relations, preserves the individual's tranquillity by keeping him on an even keel, away from either
exuberance or melancholia.

The middle way, which is the "way of the wise men," is
oriented toward the contemplative life. It is therefore somewhat more austere than an ethic that would be concerned solely
with the well-being of society. So strict a control of bodily
desire, for example, which confines desire to the needs of the
body, would not be essential for a stable community. But it is
indispensable both for "settling" the mind and for enabling the
sage to have the leisure necessary for study. The strict control
of bodily desire is a prerequisite for the Code's severe restriction upon how much work a man should do: a wise man works
only to obtain what is necessary to satisfy his immediate needs (I
4). Maimonides refers here to the proper "attitude" in acquiring money, that is, to a trait of character. The apparent
asceticism of the middle way does not preclude living in a

suitable home and having attractive possessions (III 1; cf. *Eight Chapters*, V). We should note that Maimonides assumes a sage will work at a trade or profession to support himself. A sage is forbidden to earn his livelihood by exploiting his knowledge of the Law; the Torah must not be debased by being turned into a "spade to dig with."[6] Then too, his independence is secured if he provides for his own needs. (In the Letter to Joseph included in this volume, Maimonides cautions him against accepting financial support from the Jewish authorities in Baghdad.)

There are two different standards of morality in *H. De'ot*, the middle way and piety. Although the Law commands adherence to the mean, pious men go beyond what the Law requires. They incline toward a particular extreme and are very humble, extremely generous, and so on (I 5). In the case of two character traits, piety is obligatory: a Jew is required to train himself to be extremely humble and never angry (II 3). There is accordingly a contradiction between the requirements of piety and wisdom concerning these two traits, which hints at a conflict between Jewish morality and what might be called "philosophic ethics" (cf. I 4, 5 with II 3).

The way of piety produces even greater serenity than the middle way. By requiring the elimination of every trace of arrogance, it protects people from becoming ruffled by insults. The following biblical verse is applied to those who are able to keep their composure in the face of abuse: "And those who love Him are like the sun rising in its power" (*H. De'ot*, II 3; Judges 5:13). Their indifference to insult is like the sun's indifference to any reproach that might be hurled against it as it moves across the heaven. The ultimate basis for such equanimity is alluded to later in *H. De'ot*: "According to those who understand, everything is vain and empty, and not worth taking vengeance for" (VII 7). Man's final goal is to attain knowledge of God, and the overriding importance of this goal depreciates the value of the things of this world.

The goal of knowledge of God also ennobles all activities that are instrumental for its attainment (Ch. III). If a man works to obtain what is needed to preserve his body's health so that he can attain knowledge of God, his work is regarded as serving the Lord. Human labor, in a sense disparaged here as a means, acquires dignity by being directed toward an exalted end. Even sleep serves the Lord when its purpose is to give rest to the mind and body in order to make possible the pursuit of the contemplative life.

The importance of the body's health for attaining wisdom opens the door to a detailed discussion of the care of the body (Ch. IV). It is extraordinary that within this work on ethics, Maimonides includes a regimen for health, guided by the art of medicine. Ethics is partially dependent upon the art of medicine because the middle way in bodily desire requires confining desire to what the body needs, and only the medical art can define those needs. The practice of medicine benefits from this connection with ethics because the regulation of bodily desire is itself necessary for following various medical rules, such as those regulating diet.

Maimonides considers the needs of different people in *H. De'ot*, insofar as that is possible in a law code, which is necessarily general. In Chapter Five, he proceeds to the conduct of the disciples of the wise, who have not yet attained the way of the wise men, i.e., the middle way, and therefore need a special regimen. Maimonides now uses striking metaphors to make the wrong path as repulsive as possible. For example, those who say, "Let us eat and drink, for tomorrow we die," eat from tables which are, so to speak, full of vomit (V 1); a disciple of the wise should not shout like a wild animal nor run in the street like a madman (V 7, 8); in his conjugal relations he should not behave like a rooster (V 4). The regimen for the disciple aims at overcoming whatever faults he may have. The refinement of his character also has a beneficial effect upon the whole range of his relations with other people.

In his business conduct the disciple of the wise ought to be scrupulous with himself, while showing a certain leniency toward others. He follows the rule that it is preferable for others to take advantage of him than for him to take advantage of others. His conduct in the marketplace therefore exemplifies piety (cf. V 13 with II 3); besides being indifferent to insult, he has a certain indifference to money. This attitude toward material possessions does not preclude his dressing appropriately (V 9), and he of course provides adequately for his family (V 10). He follows the rabbinic dictum to honor his family by spending more upon his wife and his children than upon himself (V 10).

The proper regulation of conversation, a recurrent theme of *H. De'ot,* is reconsidered in Chapter Five. Speech had been rather severely curtailed by an earlier rule limiting it to whatever is required for fulfilling the needs of the body or intellect (II 4). We now learn that loving-kindness is also a legitimate goal of conversation. Even here the Law tends to restrict speech, which is called for only when it would have a beneficial effect; otherwise silence is commended. Maimonides particularly emphasizes the importance of preserving peace among people and even countenances a white lie for the sake of peace. Loving-kindness takes precedence over always telling the whole truth (V 7).

The second commandment in *H. De'ot* marks the transition to the commandments that are solely for the well-being of society (VI 2). This commandment, to cleave to the wise men and their disciples, takes cognizance of the human tendency to imitate the conduct of those whom we respect. The moral education of the Code capitalizes on the traditional esteem of men who are wise and just. This implies another reason for both sage and disciple to be scrupulous in their moral conduct and indeed to be strict in obeying the Law as a whole. They must be concerned not only with their own tranquillity, but with the influence of their conduct upon other people.

The third commandment, to love your neighbor as yourself, focuses upon two of man's deepest concerns—his honor and his possessions (VI 3). It is assumed here that everyone wishes to be honored and that the individual should respect this wish in others, just as he would want his own desire for honor to be respected. Hence he should limit himself to praising his neighbor, and never disparage him. And just as a man cares for his own possessions, he should care for those of his neighbor. He is not required literally to feel the emotion of love toward other people, but to care for their honor and possessions. This interpretation overcomes the difficulty inherent in commanding someone to feel the passion of love and to love the other person to the extent that he loves himself.

The commandment, "You shall surely rebuke your neighbor," is subdivided into two parts. One refers to the situation in which an individual has been sinned against, the purpose of such a rebuke being to prevent hatred from arising in his own heart (VI 6). The second kind of rebuke aims simply at the well-being of the other person, who has either committed a sin or has followed "a way that is not good" (VI 7). The responsibility for one's fellow man inherent in this commandment presupposes a common acceptance of the Law. The concern for what the sinner (or wrongdoer) has done to his life, goes so far as to require that the attempt at correction be repeated again and again until either the admonition is accepted or the benefactor is physically assaulted.

It is forbidden to put a man to shame in public. This prohibition applies only to matters that concern a man's conduct with his fellow man, not to "matters of Heaven." By means of this distinction, Maimonides attempts to explain the public castigation of Israel by the prophets, who censured the people only for the violation of commandments involving "matters of Heaven" (VI 8).

The prohibition against being a talebearer proscribes three kinds of speech: a) the gossip of a "talebearer" (*rakhil*), in which the truth is told without defaming the other person; b) "the evil tongue," in which another person is disparaged, even though the truth is told; c) slander, in which a lie is fabricated by "one who gives his fellow man a bad name" (VII 2). Even "dust of the evil tongue"—a hint of disparaging talk—is prohibited. Now, only the first of the three kinds of proscribed speech is expressly forbidden by the Torah: "You shall not go about as a talebearer (*rakhil*) among My people" (Lev. 19:16). The other two kinds were forbidden by the rabbinic sages, whose interpretation is stricter than that found in the Torah. This difference between the biblical and rabbinic teachings helps to explain why defamation is viewed differently in *H. De'ot* than in *Eight Chapters*. The latter work commends the vilification of vicious men, although it would, strictly speaking, fall into the class of "the evil tongue." In *Eight Chapters*, Maimonides cites precedents from the Torah, not from the rabbinic tradition: the Israelites had been warned against imitating the evil deeds of the Egyptians, Canaanites, and Sodomites. Moreover he says that "virtue" requires vilifying the wicked to prevent people from falling under their influence.[7] The philosophic standard of virtue as explicated in *Eight Chapters* is more lenient than the absolute rabbinic prohibition against "the evil tongue."

The prohibition against being a talebearer is encompassed by the commandment to love your neighbor, which requires speaking only in praise of him. In fact, all the commandments that regulate man's relations with his fellow man can be subsumed under love of neighbor.[8] Thus, the last two commandments in *H. De'ot,* forbidding vengeance and bearing a grudge, are in effect corollaries of love of neighbor. The purpose of the prohibition against bearing a grudge is to make possible "the settlement of the earth and social relations among human beings" (*H. De'ot,* end).

Eight Chapters

Eight Chapters is the Introduction to Maimonides' Commentary on *Pirqei Avot* (*Chapters of the Fathers*). The health of the soul, although not neglected in *H. De'ot,* is a dominant theme of *Eight Chapters.* This can be explained by the significance piety assumes in the latter work, as indicated by the following rabbinic quotation cited by Maimonides in his Introduction: "Whoever wants to become a pious man should fulfill the words of *Avot.*" Maimonides interprets piety chiefly as a regimen for curing the diseases of the soul. Since piety is part of the prophet's self-discipline, the prophetic way of life is also examined in some detail. Here again Maimonides quotes the rabbis: "Piety brings about the holy spirit."

He presupposes, here and elsewhere, that the Jewish and philosophic traditions are distinct from one another. *Eight Chapters* appears to be an emphatically Jewish work. Nevertheless, he admittedly draws upon the work of both ancient (Greek) and modern (Islamic) philosophers. He refuses to cite his philosophic sources, however, lest a parochial reader reject a teaching because it stems from an alien work. The theme of the relation between Judaism and philosophy is therefore subdued. In comparison to *H. De'ot,* however, it is quite clearly present, for he explicitly refers to the philosophers in a number of places in *Eight Chapters* and sometimes compares their position with that of the Jewish sages. In *H. De'ot,* he never expressly speaks of the philosophers, the wise men of Greece.

Eight Chapters begins with a discussion of the human soul, tacitly based upon the works of the philosophers. (There are almost no Jewish quotations in Chapter One.) The final chapter contains an extensive discussion of a number of Jewish sources in order to show that Judaism, in agreement with philosophy, affirms human freedom. The movement from philosophy to religion, seen in an overview of the work, is repeated in most of the individual chapters, where Maimonides begins with a philo-sophic doctrine and then reconciles or compares it with the relevant Jewish teaching. (The movement from philosophy to Judaism can also be discerned in *H. De'ot* as a whole and in some of the individual chapters.)

The discussion of the human soul in Chapter One lays the groundwork for the explanation of how to cure the soul's diseases, which are found in the appetitive part of the soul. Maimonides does not confine himself to describing only the appetitive part; he gives an account of all the powers of the human soul. The rational part is thereby given its full due, being considered not from the viewpoint of the subrational, but in its own right. In fact, the appetitive part is understood from the viewpoint of the rational part. Since the intellect informs all the parts of man's soul, thereby making it a human soul, the affects of the appetitive part are, as it were, accidents of the soul.

The diseases of the soul are bad character traits, i.e., moral vices. Since they are in the appetitive part of the soul, where they are entrenched by habit, knowledge alone does not suffice to effect the cure. The sick soul must repeatedly perform actions that are opposed to his vice in order to make his character traits conform to the mean. If, for example, he is miserly, he must repeatedly be extravagant in order to achieve the middle way of liberality. If he is arrogant, he must wear tattered garments and degrade himself in various ways in the presence of other people (cf. *H. De'ot*, II 2). The repetition of the appropriate actions over a period of time can reshape the passions, producing new moral habits, so that reason can take command of the appetitive part of the soul.

Since the sick soul has a corrupt imagination and confuses good with bad actions, he needs a physician of the soul to lay down a regimen to cure him of his moral vice. Like the physician of the body, the physician of the soul "orders" the sick soul to follow the prescribed regimen. There is a fusion here of therapy and ethics: the prescription is a temporary ethic to enable the patient to acquire moral virtue.

The identification of moral virtue with the health of the soul is not arbitrary, but is a consequence of the way Maimonides conceives of health as such—for both the body and the soul. "Health is in general a certain equilibrium belonging to the domain of relation, and the privation of this relation generally constitutes illness."[9] The mean, the guideline for moral virtue, is thus also the standard for the health of the soul. Man's character traits have a basis in bodily temperaments and, like the constituents of the body in general, they are in a state of health when they are neither excessive nor deficient. To view the soul's health as lying in the mean is tantamount to saying that the healthy soul is a stable soul. Maimonides places this common-sense view into a medical context and grounds it upon the nature of the human body.

Complete health of the soul, the perfection of all the moral virtues, is rarely found. This does not imply, however, that most people have sick souls. Sickness of the soul is identical with moral vice; people with sick souls are "bad men" (Ch. III). There are two intermediate conditions between moral virtue and moral vice, namely, continence and incontinence. The continent man is tempted to do what is bad, but controls his temptation, whereas the incontinent man is tempted and succumbs.[10] Both, however, know which actions are good, whereas the sick soul has degenerated to the point where he confuses good with bad actions. The sick soul is especially in need of a physician of the soul to prescribe a course of treatment.

Piety, which entails inclining toward an extreme, is a therapeutic method for curing the diseases of the soul. It is also a precautionary measure against allowing moral vice to enter surreptitiously into the soul. Such a safeguard is needed because moral vice may develop slowly and, at first, imperceptibly in the soul.

The Law fulfills a similar pedagogic and therapeutic purpose, for it requires people to incline toward the extreme in order to train them to achieve the middle way in ethics. It does not take into account, however, the distinctive needs of a particular individual, which could only be done by a physician of the soul. The Law must be distinguished from the art of medicine, which treats diseases on an individual basis.[11] Nevertheless, the Law does take into account what may be called typical vices and prescribes a discipline for the entire community.

Although the Law lays down a strict discipline, it does not countenance the excesses of asceticism, a point emphasized by Maimonides to forestall any misunderstanding that might result from his teaching that going toward the extreme can be salutary. He does not recommend afflicting the body to cure the soul's diseases. He reiterates his opposition to asceticism when he turns to the prophetic, or contemplative, way of life (Ch. V). In fact, he now says that beautiful surroundings and even decorative clothes can be justified to dispel the melancholia that might accompany the solitary contemplative life. For therapeutic purposes, Maimonides recommends walking in beautiful gardens, looking at beautiful objects, and listening to music. Beauty is understood as a means to an end, as instrumental to the intellect's need for a joyful state of mind.

The prophet's ultimate goal, like that of the wise man, is the intellectual perception of God. Although this goal is discussed briefly (in Chapter Seven), *Eight Chapters* is concerned with the prophetic way of life, not with prophecy as such. As a work on ethics, it has a practical intent, laying down a way of life which, in principle, can be followed at any time. Maimonides does not assume that prophecy ceased forever with the close of the biblical period, but that it is an ever present possibility for men with the appropriate gifts and training.

The prophet's life is brought into order, it is given a focus, by being directed toward a single goal (Ch. V). This goal, to attain knowledge of God, reorients the earlier discussion of the health of the soul. A healthy soul is not an end in itself, but a means for the well-being of the intellect. Moreover, from this new vantage point, the standard of the mean is seen to be just a rough guideline, satisfactory only within a limited horizon. The contemplative life requires an extreme kind of devotion, subordinating everything else to its own purpose. If it strikes a mean at all, the "excess" of contemplation is balanced by a "deficiency" of other activities. A man's actions and conversation are severely curtailed when guided by the goal of contemplation (Ch. V).

It is in this context that Maimonides forcefully condemns hedonism. If intellectual perception is the goal of human life, bodily pleasure becomes incidental. Man's ultimate goal requires a concern with the body's health rather than its pleasure.

Toward the end of Chapter Five, Maimonides hints that the all-encompassing contemplative goal might occasionally conflict with the demands of the Law. He resolves this difficulty by appealing to a rabbinic teaching that sanctions a transgression when committed in obedience to the dictum: "In all your ways know Him" (Prov. 3:6). At this point, Maimonides says the goal is the truth.

Chapters Six through Eight aim at reconciling the Jewish tradition with some of the philosophic doctrines that had been explicated or presupposed earlier in *Eight Chapters*. In Chapter Six, Maimonides examines certain rabbinic statements which apparently contradict the philosophic view that a virtuous man never desires to do anything bad and is simply superior to a continent man. In order to reconcile the apparent contradiction between Judaism and philosophy, he distinguishes between "traditions" and "generally accepted opinions." When the rabbis laud someone who desires something bad but conquers his desire, they refer only to the desire for things prohibited by the particular tradition of the Jewish nation, such as mixing milk and meat, illicit sexual unions, etc. The man who successfully struggles to control his desire to transgress "traditions" is superior to one who is never even tempted. Judaism is in agreement with philosophy that the desire to violate "generally accepted opinions," such as prohibitions against murder, theft, etc., is always wrong.

When Maimonides had spoken earlier of the moral vices as diseases of the soul, he had presupposed the philosophic understanding of the subject.[12] In Chapter Seven he shows how the moral vices are viewed by the prophets. He quotes from Isaiah, who refers not to "moral vices" but to "sins" that separate man from God. Seen though the eyes of prophecy, the moral vices are like veils that hinder the contemplation of God.

From a philosophic standpoint, the question of whether man

is free turns upon the nature of his "inborn disposition" (*fiṭrah*), or temperament, which has an effect upon traits of character and intellect. Since the "inborn disposition" is subject to habituation and training, man is able to become virtuous or wicked. This doctrine, based upon reason and observation, is in agreement with the premise of the Law concerning human freedom. Judaism, however, does not speak with an unambiguous voice on this subject. How are we to understand certain biblical statements—such as the reference to God's hardening Pharaoh's heart—that seem to deny human freedom? Such questions of exegesis are inseparable from the "theological" problem of how God's omniscience can be reconciled with human freedom. Maimonides discusses the cluster of problems surrounding human freedom in Chapter Eight.

On the Management of Health

In this work Maimonides applies his view of therapy to the problems of a particular individual, the Sultan al-Afḍal, who had requested advice on how to cure his anxiety and depression. Maimonides' reply includes broad counsel on how to cure the diseases of the soul. Since the sultan had also complained of bodily ailments, Maimonides emphasizes the interdependence of body and soul. A disordered state of the passions—which have a bodily basis—affects the health of the body. Maimonides singles out depression as producing bodily symptoms, and he advises physicians in general to see first of all that their patients have a cheerful frame of mind.

The medical art does not provide the knowledge necessary for healing the diseases of the soul. Maimonides recognizes two sources of treatment: religion and practical philosophy. Both utilize essentially the same therapeutic method of compelling the sick soul to follow a regimen opposed to its vice. Besides the discipline imposed by religion, its therapeutic value derives from maxims, admonitions, and edifying tales.

In this work, intended to meet the difficulties of a ruler whose power and wealth were subject to great change, Maimonides teaches that a healthy soul is neither excessively joyful at good fortune nor depressed by bad fortune. The therapy consists in training the soul to become less and less affected by either good or bad fortune. Maimonides minimizes the importance of material goods by referring to their transitory character, and he completely deflates the significance of any worldly loss by comparing it to the finality of death. It is clearer in this work than in *Eight Chapters* that the opinions held by people affect the health of the soul. Maimonides emphasizes here the need to distinguish between imaginary and true happiness, though he only briefly alludes to the religious conception of eternal happiness, and does not further elaborate his view of true happiness.

As in *Eight Chapters*, we see that the imagination plays havoc with the sick soul, deceiving him into magnifying either good or bad fortune, causing him to grieve about things past, and making him fearful of the future. Health includes the recognition that what has happened in the past cannot be changed and that future events cannot be known and hence should not be feared. The misery of the sick soul is not regarded as simply bad, for distress can serve a useful purpose by forcing an individual to acquire moral virtue and to devote himself to the worship of God.

Letter to Joseph

The letter to Joseph ben Judah included in this volume is important for many reasons. It gives information about Maimonides' support of the Exilarch, a "secular" leader, and the concomitant opposition to Samuel ben Ali, the religious head of Babylonian Jewry; it helps to date the *Guide of the Perplexed*; it indicates that Maimonides did not study the works of Averroes until the *Guide* was substantially complete. This letter also shows the political acumen of Maimonides in dealing with a cunning foe, Samuel ben Ali, and throws light upon the relevance of ethics ("moral habits") to political controversy.

Maimonides' disciple, Joseph, had become embroiled in a controversy with Samuel ben Ali and had been vilified by Samuel and his associates. Maimonides urges Joseph to conduct himself with humility in this dispute. As a model for Joseph, Maimonides refers to his own humility; he had trained himself to remain calm in the face of abuse. Maimonides would preserve his equanimity no matter what the provocation. His humility is accompanied by a nobility that would prevent him from replying in kind to the insults of fools, among whom Maimonides numbers Samuel ben Ali.

In this letter Maimonides reveals his sobriety, his lack of sentimentality, in judging human beings. He had anticipated the attacks of arrogant, envious men upon his monumental work, the *Mishneh Torah*. He was not surprised that the Code was belittled by Samuel ben Ali, nor that the latter had behaved badly toward Joseph. Samuel's character had been shaped from childhood by the expectation of praise and admiration. And now his authority and prestige were threatened by Joseph's plans to establish a school in which the basis of instruction would be Maimonides' Code. Joseph also seems to have been instrumental in protecting the independence of the Exilarchate against Samuel's attempt to control it. Joseph lacked the experience and judgment of his teacher, who attempts to open his disciple's eyes to the ways of the world. Did Joseph expect Samuel to be grateful for curbing his ambition and demeaning his authority?

Maimonides moves on a number of fronts to assuage Joseph's anger and to urge him to treat Samuel with respect. Joseph's agitation prevents him from spending his time profitably. A lifetime could be wasted if one attempted to correct the errors of every ignoramus. Maimonides also appeals to Joseph's duty to obey his teacher and to put an end to the dispute. Moreover, Joseph is reminded that Jewish law requires honoring an elder, and all the more, one who heads a school. At the same time, Maimonides expresses contempt for Samuel, thereby removing the sting from the latter's harsh attacks upon Joseph. Samuel's words hardly deserve to be taken seriously.

Maimonides also had to deal with Samuel ben Ali and did so with great tact. One facet of his prudence is revealed by what he had written to Samuel, as reported in the letter to Joseph, in response to the charge that Joseph had called Samuel an old fool. Maimonides replied: "Those who say such things are gossipmongers; he [Joseph] would not think it permissible to do something like that. In his letter, which is in my hands, he praises you and says that there is no one like you in Iraq"(#13). Although the letter from Joseph is not extant, Maimonides obviously made a slight change by reporting that Joseph had "praised" Samuel ben Ali when writing that there was no one like him in the whole of Iraq. We are reminded that, according to *H. De'ot*, although lying is generally forbidden, an exception is made for "matters concerning peace" (V 7).

Guide of the Perplexed
and Treatise on the Art of Logic

In *Eight Chapters* (VI), Maimonides condemns those who believe in "rational laws" for governing human conduct as suffering from the sickness of the Mutakallimūn (dialectical theologians). He himself affirms the existence of "generally accepted opinions." We postponed discussion of this issue in our earlier analysis of *Eight Chapters* in order to be able to deal with it in the context of the selections from the *Guide* and the *Logic*.

Maimonides distinguishes between generally accepted opinions and intelligibles. Whereas the former are concerned with the noble and the base, the latter deal with truth and falsehood. Generally accepted opinions regulate human actions, which are properly called noble or base, rather than true or false. Knowledge of nature is acquired through intelligibles. Generally accepted opinions are based not upon nature but upon the tacit or explicit agreement of human beings. They do not refer to what is right by nature.[13]

When the Mutakallimūn speak about "rational laws," or more precisely, "intellectual laws" (*al-sharā'i' al-'aqlīyah*), they confuse the difference between an intelligible (*ma'qūl*) and a law. Since law has the form of a commandment, it is not qua command concerned with truth and falsehood. A law is therefore not as such an intelligible. Now, it is possible for knowledge to be required by law, and in such cases a certain ambiguity arises. The knowledge itself would be an intelligible, though the law as such would not. Thus the first two of the Ten Commandments, which require knowledge of God's existence and unity respectively, refer to intelligibles (*Guide*, II 33). Since, however, a commandment cannot itself be an intelligible, the classification of such laws is ambiguous.[14] In conformity with his opposition to the Mutakallimūn, Maimonides classifies the other eight of the Ten Commandments as either generally accepted opinions or traditions.

According to *Eight Chapters* (VI), it is generally accepted that the following are bad: murder, theft, robbery, fraud, harming the innocent, repaying good with evil, and the degrading of parents. A decent community calls for certain elementary restraints, as attested to by the common sense of mankind. Since the above opinions are useful for the well-being of any society, they have a loose connection with man's political nature. They are not necessarily found among all peoples, however, for they derive from human consensus. Moreover, they are not valid for all men under all possible circumstances. Necessity can be ascribed to intelligibles, but not to generally accepted opinions. "With regard to what is of necessity, there is no good or evil at all, only the false and the true" (*Guide*, I 2).

The loose connection of the above opinions with human nature explains their widespread acceptance, without requiring that they be either universally accepted or universally valid. Man's political nature is the ground for the recognition among most, if not all, nations of virtually the same opinions as eminently useful for the community. The broad acceptance of these opinions also presupposes that people living under different conditions at different times are all capable of distinguishing between the noble and the base. Maimonides regards this capability as present in man by nature.[15] Only the capacity to judge is given by nature. He tacitly denies the existence of a conscience (or *synderesis*) containing the precepts of practical reason. At the same time, he takes cognizance of the extent to which certain elementary rules of justice are found among the human race.

Since he regards the middle way as right by nature, we are led to consider briefly what relationship, if any, there is between generally accepted opinions and the moral virtues. First we must recognize that whereas the former regulate human actions, the latter are noble character traits that refer to a certain order within the human soul. Now, if someone possesses moral virtue, he would not wish to transgress the generally accepted opinions (*Eight Chapters*, VI). But possession of moral virtue is not a *sine qua non* for following these opinions. If it were, the bonds of society would be extraordinarily fragile, for complete moral virtue is rarely found. It is true that moral virtue requires fulfilling various duties to other people (*Guide*, III 53). But Maimonides gives no indication that such duties are identical with generally accepted opinions. The latter are grounded not upon moral virtue but upon human consensus.

Although generally accepted opinions are usually formulated as laws, they strictly refer to the noble and the base (or the good and the bad); they therefore need not have the force of law. Thus it is generally recognized that to recompense a benefactor generously is noble (*Logic*, VIII). Nobility has to be distinguished from what is obligatory, which is determined by law. It is also distinct from necessity, which is applicable to intelligibles, to the domain of truth and falsehood.

In his discussion of logical modalities, Maimonides distinguishes between nobility on the one hand and both obligation and necessity on the other. Among the modalities recognized by him are the following: "It is noble (for)," "It is base (for)," "It is obligatory," and "It is necessary" (*Logic*, III). It is noteworthy that Maimonides formulates the noble and the base as modalities.[16] In the proposition, "It is noble for David to be generous," the modality shows how the generosity of David is to be characterized. A modality, according to Maimonides, shows how the predicate is related to the subject of a proposition. For this reason even the noble and the base can be treated as modalities. If, however, a modality were understood as determining the value of the copula "is" (as in Kantian philosophy), there would be no such modalities. It would not be proper to say, "David nobly is generous," although one could say, "The earth necessarily is round." But our main point here is that Maimonides' treatment of modalities consorts with his view of generally accepted opinions.

Besides generally accepted opinions, human conduct is governed by "traditions," which are usually distinctive of only one or perhaps a few nations. It is also possible for a generally accepted opinion to be found in only one or a few nations, but its utility is always self-evident. The reasons for traditions are not obvious. Traditions are "what is received" (*al-maqbūlāt*: *ha-mequbalot*); their validity stems from having been "received" from an authoritative individual or assembly (*Logic*, VIII). Although their usefulness is at first glance obscure, Maimonides attempts, wherever possible, to justify them on grounds of utility. They can for instance serve as a discipline for correcting certain vices, as in the case of the prohibition concerning "forbidden foods," which aims at curbing the vice of gluttony (*Eight Chapters*, IV). Different traditions, found among different peoples, can presumably serve the same end. But a particular tradition, no matter where it is found, might not be salutary for all the people obliged to follow it. The ground for the obedience of traditions cannot be mere utility.

Maimonides' rejection of the existence of "rational laws" implies that neither generally accepted opinions nor traditions are demonstrable. In the *Logic* (VIII), he says that neither kind of premise requires a proof. In this respect, they are similar to the propositions embodying first intelligibles and sense perceptions which, as the ultimate premises of the theoretical sciences, are not themselves demonstrable. The fundamental premises of both practical and theoretical argumentation are not amenable to proof. They are all ultimately "given," though the first intelligibles and sense perceptions are given in a manner quite different from the basic premises governing human conduct. The premises of the theoretical sciences are given by nature to everyone whose intellect and senses are sound.

The rejection of "rational laws" does not imply that there are no reasons for the commandments. The reasons are more precisely "causes" in the sense of "final causes" or purposes. The commandments, though not inherently rational, can be justified as useful for achieving certain goals. The ends, in contradistinction to the means, are regarded by Maimonides as demonstrable. The ends of the Law are the well-being of the intellect and the body, with the body's well-being understood to require a well-ordered community. Succinctly stated, the Law teaches correct opinions, instills good moral habits, and prevents wrongdoing (*Guide*, III 27). Since the ends of the Law are given by nature, it can be said of the Law that "although it is not natural, it has a connection with [or a portal to] what is natural" (*Guide*, II 40).

Although there are no "rational laws," there is a hierarchy of natural ends. The same ends that justify the Law can provide guidance for the individual's deliberation concerning particular decisions. In this way Maimonides appears to overcome the possible conflict between what might be required by the Law on the one hand and deliberation independent of the Law on the other. When man's needs are considered with a view to their dignity, the human goods can be placed in the following order, ascending from the least to the most important: possessions, bodily health, moral virtue, and intellectual virtue (*Guide*, III 54). A rational decision would have to take into account the exigencies of life and consider the urgency as well as the dignity of the goods in question.

The Days of the Messiah

Since there are no "rational laws" for governing human life, there is no single political order that reason can specify as best for every community. Maimonides never discusses the best regime as such, in the manner, say, of Plato in the *Republic*. He does describe the best *Jewish* regime in his account of the messianic era. This account is at once more "parochial" and more "universal" than Plato's view of justice described in the *Republic*. It is more "parochial" because its articulation is guided by the beliefs of a particular nation; it also expresses distinctively Jewish concerns, especially the elimination of Jewish suffering in the Exile. It is more "universal" in the sense that it is not confined to a single polity, but encompasses the entire world: the messianic era, as envisaged by the prophets, is a time of peace among the nations. Maimonides' view of the end of days is not altogether alien to the thought of Plato, however, for the ultimate purpose of the messianic era is to enable men to pursue the contemplative life. Moreover, world peace will be brought about by a prophet-king who is reminiscent of Plato's philosopher-king. The messiah will combine extraordinary wisdom with political rule, which calls to mind Plato's view that the best regime can come into existence only if philosophers become kings or kings become philosophers.[17]

The nations of the world will be attracted to the messiah because of his great wisdom and consummate justice.[18] Jesus and Muhammad have already helped to lay the groundwork for the messianic era by directing a large portion of mankind toward the service of God.[19] The messianic king will correct their mistakes and teach the nations the true way of the Lord.[20] He will have to be not only a teacher, but also a political leader, indeed a statesman with great military skill. For peaceful means will not suffice to unify the nations and to usher in the messianic era. The messiah will have to engage in warfare, and his success in battle will be one of the signs that he is in fact the messianic king.[21] On the whole, Maimonides gives a "naturalistic" account of how the messianic era will come into existence.[22]

According to *Laws of Kings and Their Wars*, the Temple will be rebuilt and the sacrificial cult restored in the messianic era, but they are not mentioned in the account in *Laws Concerning Repentance*. One is reminded that according to the *Guide*, the sacrificial cult was established by Mosaic law as a concession to the habits of the ancient Hebrews, who had been accustomed to associating worship with sacrifice because of the common practice of their day.[23] Whether the sacrificial cult would have to be restored if people are no longer accustomed to bring sacrifices could be questioned.[24] Be that as it may, Maimonides says in *Laws of Kings* that the entire Torah, including the sacrificial laws, will be obeyed in the days of the messiah.

He emphasizes that the course of nature ("the custom of the world") will not change during the days of the messiah. There will still be differences in intellectual capacity, and the knowledge of God will vary from individual to individual. All people will have the leisure to study the Torah and its wisdom. The intellectual perpetuity of the afterlife, however, is attained through wisdom simply.[25] Besides the inequality of the intellect, there will still be an inequality of material possessions. He replies in *Pereq Ḥeleq* to a hypothetical question on this subject as follows: "In his [the messiah's] days, the powerful and the weak will [still] be distinguished from one another."[26] However, the elimination of oppression in the Exile will ease the hardship of earning a livelihood. In any event, the inequality of possessions will have no importance for those engaged in the pursuit of knowledge.

Since human nature will not be transformed, the Law will still be needed for moral training and the prevention of injustice. Although Maimonides is intentionally vague about the future global political order, he articulates the prophetic vision that mankind will remain divided into nations. A single religion will serve as the bond that unites them. Peace among individuals and nations will be furthered by an abundance of material goods.[27] The promise of peace held out by Scripture is mainly based, however, upon the vision of a universal preoccupation with attaining knowledge of the deity, a goal that eliminates every reason for people to harm one another.[28] The love of wisdom places humankind beyond the lure of moral vice.[29] While moral virtue is instrumental for the contemplative life, the reverse is also true. Contemplation itself aids in preserving moral excellence.

NOTES

1. Maimonides, *Maqālah fī Bayān Ba'd al-A'raḍ wa al-Jawāb 'anhā (Treatise on the Clarification of Some Accidents. . .)*, ed. H. Kroner (Leiden: Brill, 1928), p. 53; English trans. by A. Bar-Sela, H. Hoff, and E. Faris, in *Transactions of the American Philosophical Society*, LIV, 4 (July 1964), p. 40.
2. Joseph Kaspi on *Guide*, II 40.
3. *Guide*, II 40, *infra*, pp. 134-35.
4. *Mishneh Torah*, Laws of the Foundations of the Torah, IV 13. A man's tranquillity of mind *(yishuv da'ato)* as well as his intellectual capacity determine whether he should study the theoretical sciences *(pardes)*, after he has mastered Jewish law (Laws of the Study of the Torah, I 12). The *Mishneh Torah* is cited henceforth as *M.T.*
5. *Guide*, III 39 (85b).
6. *Mishnah*, Avot, IV 7; *M.T.*, Laws of the Study of the Torah, III 10.
7. *Commentary on the Mishnah*, Eight Chapters, V. *infra*, pp. 76-77. The *Commentary on the Mishnah* is cited henceforth as *C.M.*
8. Cf. *C.M.*, Pe'ah, I 1.
9. *Guide*, III 10 (16b).
10. *C.M.*, Eight Chapters, VI. Maimonides speaks there only of continence. For a discussion of both continence and incontinence, see Aristotle, *Nicomachean Ethics*, Book VII.
11. See *infra*, *Guide*, III 34.
12. The philosophers understand the soul as being healthy or sick. See *C.M.*, Eight Chapters, III, note one.

13. For a detailed discussion of this issue, see Leo Strauss, *Persecution and the Art of Writing* (Glencoe: Free Press, 1952), pp. 95–141; *What Is Political Philosophy?* (Glencoe: Free Press, 1959), pp. 166–67.
14. *C.M.*, Eight Chapters, II, *infra*, pp. 64-65.
15. *C.M.*, Eight Chapters, I, *infra*, p. 63.
16. Cf. *Alfarabi's Commentary on Aristotle's De Interpretatione*, Arabic text ed. by W. Kutsch and S. Marrow (Beirut: Catholic Press, 1960), p. 163.
17. Leo Strauss has shown the general significance of Plato for Maimonides' conception of prophecy. See, e.g., *Philosophie und Gesetz* (Berlin: Schocken, 1935), p. 108ff.
18. *C.M.*, Pereq Heleq, *infra*, p. 166.
19. *M.T.*, Laws of Kings and Their Wars, XI 4.
20. *M.T.*, Laws Concerning Repentance, IX 9.
21. *M.T.*, Laws of Kings and Their Wars, XI 1, 4; XII 2.
22. He does refer occasionally to the miracles that will appear through the messiah. See *C.M.*, Pereq Heleq, *infra*, p. 166 and note three *ad loc.*
23. *Guide*, III 32.
24. Cf. *ibid.* (70a).
25. Cf. *M.T.*, Laws of Kings and Their Wars, XII 4, with Laws Concerning Repentance, IX 8.
26. *C.M.*, Pereq Heleq, *infra*, p. 166 and note five *ad loc.* (Kafih, pp. 197, 207).
27. *M.T.*, Laws of Kings and Their Wars, XII 5; cf. *C.M.*, Pereq Heleq, *infra*, p. 166.
28. *Guide*, III 11, *infra*, p. 177.
29. *C.M.*, Pereq Heleq, *infra*, p. 168.

I

LAWS CONCERNING
CHARACTER TRAITS

Laws Concerning Character Traits (*Hilkhot De'ot*) is part of The Book of Knowledge, the first of the fourteen books in Maimonides' monumental Code, the *Mishneh Torah*. The Code brings lucid order to the vastness of Jewish law by classifying laws according to subject. It is a compilation of the Oral Law, as distinct from the Written Law of the Pentateuch. The Oral Law, according to Maimonides, was originally handed down by Moses and ultimately recorded in the *Babylonian* and *Jerusalem Talmuds* as well as other rabbinic works. Maimonides regards his codification of the Oral Law as an explanation of the Written Law. Thus, in *H. De'ot* he explicates eleven commandments from the Torah.

The title, *Laws of De'ot,* cannot be adequately rendered in English. The word *de'ah* (pl. *de'ot*) is derived from the Hebrew root "to know" and usually means "knowledge" or "opinion." In the *Mishneh Torah*, it has a variety of meanings, including "knowledge" as well as "intellect." In *H. De'ot, de'ah* refers to a state of mind, an attitude with respect to a passion, and is translated as "character trait."

The division into paragraphs follows that of the Bodleian manuscript edited by Hyamson, which was corrected on the basis of Maimonides' own text. The numbers in square brackets are not in the original Hebrew text; they indicate the division into sections found in the traditional versions.

LAWS CONCERNING
CHARACTER TRAITS

They include altogether eleven commandments, five positive commandments and six negative commandments. These are: 1) to imitate His ways, 2) to cleave to those who know Him, 3) to love neighbors, 4) to love the converts, 5) not to hate brothers, 6) to rebuke, 7) not to put [anyone] to shame, 8) not to afflict the distressed, 9) not to go about as a talebearer, 10) not to take revenge, 11) not to bear a grudge.[1] The explanation of all these commandments is in the following chapters.

CHAPTER ONE

[1] Every single human being[2] has many character traits. [As for character traits in general,] one differs from another and they are exceedingly far apart from each other. One man is irascible, perpetually angry, and another man has a tranquil mind and does not become angry at all; if he does become angry, his anger is mild and only rarely aroused during a period of several years. One man has an exceedingly haughty heart, and another has an extremely lowly spirit. One is so full of desire that his soul is never satisfied by pursuing its desire; another has a body so exceedingly pure that he does not even desire the few things the body needs. One has a desire[3] so great that his soul would not be satisfied with all the wealth in the world. As it is said: "He that loves silver shall not be satisfied with silver."[4] Another is so constrained that he would be satisfied with some small thing not adequate for him, and he does not press to acquire whatever he needs.

One torments himself with hunger and is so tightfisted that he does not eat the worth of a small coin except when in great pain; another intentionally squanders all his wealth. All the rest of the character traits follow these patterns, which are [also] exemplified by the gay and the mournful, the miserly and the prodigal, the cruel and the merciful, the soft-hearted and the hard-hearted, and so on.[5]

[2] Between two character traits at opposite extremes, there is a character trait in the middle, equidistant from the extremes. Some character traits a man has from the beginning of his

creation,[6] depending upon the nature of his body; some character traits a certain man's nature is disposed to receive in the future more quickly than other character traits; and some a man does not have from the beginning of his creation[6] but learns from others, or he himself turns to them due to a thought that arose in his heart, or he hears that a certain character trait is good for him and that it is proper to acquire it and he trains himself in it until it is firmly established within him.

[3] For any character trait, the two opposite extremes are not the good way, and it is not proper for a man to follow them nor to teach them to himself. If he finds his nature inclined toward one extreme or if he is disposed to receive one of them or if he has already learned one of them and has become accustomed to it, he shall make himself return to the good way and follow the way of good men, which is the right way.[7]

[4] The right way[7] is the mean[8] in every single one of a man's character traits. It is the character trait that is equally distant from the two extremes, not close to one or the other. Therefore the wise men of old[9] commanded that a man continuously appraise his character traits and evaluate them and direct them in the middle way so that he becomes perfect.[10]

How so? A man shall not be irascible and easily angered, nor like a corpse which feels nothing, but in between; he shall only become angry about a large matter that deserves anger so that something like it not be done again.

So too, he shall only desire the things which the body needs and without which it is impossible to live. As it is said: "A just man eats to satisfy his desire."[11] Likewise, he shall only labor at his work to acquire what he needs for the present. As it is said: "Good is a little for the just man."[12] He shall not be exceedingly tightfisted, nor squander all his wealth, but he shall give charity according to his means and lend a fitting amount to the needy. He shall not be gay and buffoonish nor sad and mournful, but rejoice all his days, calmly, with a cheerful demeanor. And thus shall he order the rest of his character traits. This way is the way of the wise men.

Every man whose character traits all lie in the mean is called a wise man. [5] Whoever is exceedingly scrupulous with himself and moves a little toward one side or the other, away from the character trait in the mean, is called a pious man.

How so? Whoever moves away from a haughty heart to the

opposite extreme so that he is exceedingly lowly in spirit is called a pious man; this is the measure of piety. If he moves only to the mean and is humble, he is called a wise man; this is the measure of wisdom. The same applies to all the rest of the character traits. The pious men of old[13] used to direct their character traits from the middle way toward [one of] the two extremes; some character traits toward the last extreme, and some toward the first extreme. This is the meaning of "inside the line of the law."[14]

We are commanded to walk in these middle ways, which are the good and right[15] ways. As it is said: "And you shall walk in His ways."[16] [6] Thus they taught in explaining this commandment: Just as He is called gracious, you too be gracious; just as He is called merciful, you too be merciful; just as He is called holy, you too be holy.[17]

In like manner, the prophets applied all these terms to God: slow to anger and abundant in loving-kindness, just and righteous,[18] perfect, powerful, strong, and the like. They did so to proclaim that these ways are good and right,[19] and a man is obliged to train himself to follow them and to imitate[20] according to his strength.

[7] How so? A man shall habituate himself in these character traits until they are firmly established in him. Time after time, he shall perform actions in accordance with the character traits that are in the mean. He shall repeat them continually until performing them is easy for him and they are not burdensome and these character traits are firmly established in his soul.

Since these terms applied to the Creator[21] refer to the middle way that we are obliged to follow, this way is called the way of the Lord. That is what Abraham taught to his sons. As it is said: "For I have known him so that he will command his sons and his household after him to keep the way of the Lord, to do justice and righteousness."[22] Whoever walks in this way brings good and blessing upon himself. As it is said: "In order that the Lord render unto Abraham that which He said concerning him."[23]

CHAPTER TWO

[1] Those whose bodies are sick taste the bitter as sweet and the sweet as bitter. Some of the sick desire and long for foods

that are not fit to eat, such as soil and charcoal, and they hate good foods, such as bread and meat. It all depends upon the extent of the illness. Likewise, people with sick souls crave and love the bad character traits and hate the good way. They are careless about following it, and it is very difficult for them, depending upon the extent of their illness. Thus says Isaiah about these men: "Woe unto them who call evil good, and good evil; who turn darkness into light, and light into darkness; who turn the bitter into the sweet, and the sweet into the bitter."[1] Of them it is said: "They forsake the paths of righteousness to walk in the ways of darkness."[2]

What is the remedy for those whose souls are sick? Let them go to the wise men—who are physicians of the soul—and they will cure their disease by means of the character traits that they shall teach them, until they make them return to the middle way. Solomon said about those who recognize their bad character traits and do not go to the wise men to be cured: "Fools despise admonition."[3]

[2] How are they to be cured? Whoever is irascible is told to train himself so that if he is beaten and cursed, he will not feel anything. He shall follow this way for a long time until the rage is uprooted from his heart. If his heart is haughty, he shall train himself to endure much degradation. He shall sit lower than anyone else and wear worn-out, shabby garments, which make the wearer despised, and do similar things, until his haughty heart is uprooted. Then he shall return to the middle way, which is the good way, and when he returns to the middle way he shall follow it all his days.

He shall do the same with all the other character traits. If he is at one extreme, he shall move to the other extreme and accustom himself to it for a long time until he returns to the good way, which is the mean[4] in every single character trait.

[3] In the case of some character traits, a man is forbidden to accustom himself to the mean. Rather, he shall move to the other [i.e., far] extreme. One such [character trait] is a haughty heart, for the good way is not that a man be merely humble, but that he have a lowly spirit, that his spirit be very submissive.[5] Therefore it was said of Moses our master that he was "very humble," and not merely humble.[6] And therefore the wise men commanded: "Have a very, very lowly spirit."[7] Moreover they said that everyone who makes his heart haughty denies the

existence of God.[8] As it is said: "And your heart shall swell, and you shall forget the Lord your God."[9] In addition they said: "Whoever has an arrogant spirit—even a little—deserves excommunication."[10] Likewise, anger is an extremely bad character trait, and it is proper for a man to move away from it to the other extreme and to teach himself not to become angry, even over something it is proper to be angry about. Now, he might wish to arouse fear in his children and the members of his household or in the community (if he is a leader) and to become angry at them in order that they return to what is good. Then he shall pretend to be angry in their presence in order to admonish them, but his mind shall be tranquil within himself, like a man who feigns anger but is not angry. The wise men of old[11] said: "Anyone who is angry—it is as if he worships idols."[12] They said about anyone who is angry: If he is a wise man, his wisdom departs from him, and if he is a prophet, his prophecy departs from him.[13] And [they said] the life of irascible men is no life.[14] Therefore they commanded a man to refrain from becoming angry, until he trains himself not to feel anything even in response to things that provoke anger; this is the good way. The way of the just men is to be insulted but not to insult; they hear themselves reviled and do not reply; they act out of love and rejoice in afflictions. Scripture says about them: "And those who love Him are like the sun rising in its power."[15]

[4] There shall always be much silence in a man's conduct. He shall speak only about a matter concerned with wisdom or matters that are necessary to keep his body alive. They said about Rav, a student of our holy master, that during his entire life he did not engage in idle conversation.[16] The latter is characteristic of most men. A man shall not use many words, even in connection with the needs of the body. Concerning this, the wise men commanded, saying: "Anyone who multiplies words brings about sin."[17] They also said: "I have found nothing better for the body than silence."[18] Likewise, concerning words of Torah and words of wisdom, the words of the wise man shall be few, but full of content. This is what the wise men commanded, saying: "A man shall always teach his students by the shortest path."[19] But if the words are many and the content slight, that is indeed foolishness. Concerning this it is said: "For

a dream comes with much content, but a fool's voice with many words."[20]

[5] Silence is a fence around wisdom.[21] Therefore he shall not hasten to reply, nor speak much; he shall teach his students quietly and calmly, without shouting or prolixity. That is in keeping with the saying of Solomon: "Words of wise men, spoken calmly, are listened to."[22]

[6] A man is forbidden to make a habit of using smooth and deceptive language. There shall not be one thing in his mouth and another in his heart, but what is within shall be like what is without. The matter in his heart shall be the same as what is in his mouth. It is forbidden to delude[23] one's fellow creatures, even a Gentile.

How so? He shall not sell to a Gentile meat not ritually slaughtered as though it were ritually slaughtered, nor a shoe made from an animal that died by itself in place of one ritually slaughtered. He shall not urge his friend to eat with him when he knows he will not eat, nor press refreshment upon him when he knows it will not be accepted, nor open casks of wine (which he needs to open to sell anyway) to deceive him into thinking they were opened to honor him. Likewise with everything like that—even one word of deception and fraud is forbidden. Rather, he shall have lips of truth, a steadfast spirit, and a heart pure of all mischief and intrigue.

[7] A man shall not be full of laughter and mockery, nor sad and mournful, but joyful. Thus the wise men said: "Laughter and levity bring about illicit sexual conduct."[24] They commanded that a man not be unrestrained in laughter, nor sad and mournful, but that he receive every man with a cheerful demeanor.[25] Likewise his desire[26] shall not be so great that he rushes for wealth, nor shall he be lazy and refrain from working. But he shall live in contentment,[27] have a modest occupation, and be occupied [mainly] with the Torah.[28] No matter how small his portion, let him rejoice in it.[29] He shall not be full of contention, envy, or desire, nor shall he seek honor. Thus the wise men said: "Envy, desire, and honor remove a man from the world."[30] The general rule is that he follow the mean[31] for every single character trait, until all his character traits are ordered according to the mean. That is in keeping with what Solomon says: "And all your ways will be upright."[32]

CHAPTER THREE

[1] Perhaps a man will say: "Since desire, honor, and the like constitute a bad way and remove a man from the world, I shall completely separate myself from them and go to the other extreme." So he does not eat meat, nor drink wine, nor take a wife, nor live in a decent[1] dwelling, nor wear decent[1] clothing, but sackcloth, coarse wool, and so on, like the priests of Edom.[2] This, too, is a bad way and it is forbidden to follow it.

Whoever follows this way is called a sinner. Indeed, He [God] says about the Nazirite: "He [the priest] shall make atonement for him because he sinned against the soul."[3] The wise men said: "If the Nazirite who only abstained from wine needs atonement, how much more does one who abstains from every thing [need atonement]."[4]

Therefore the wise men commanded that a man only abstain from things forbidden by the Torah alone. He shall not prohibit for himself, by vows and oaths, things that are permitted. Thus the wise men said: "Is what the Torah has prohibited not enough for you, that you prohibit other things for yourself?"[5]

Those who fast continually are in this class; they do not follow the good way. The wise men prohibited a man from tormenting himself by fasting. Concerning all these things and others like them, Solomon commanded, saying: "Do not be overly righteous and do not be excessively wise; why should you destroy yourself?"[6]

[2] Man[7] needs to direct every single one of his deeds solely toward attaining knowledge of the Name, blessed be He. His sitting down, his standing up, and his speech, everything shall be directed toward this goal. How so? When he conducts business or works to receive a wage, his heart shall not only be set upon taking in money, but he shall do these things in order to acquire what the body needs, such as food, drink, shelter, and a wife.

Likewise when he eats, drinks, and has sexual intercourse, his purpose[8] shall not be to do these things only for pleasure, eating and drinking only what is sweet to the palate and having sexual intercourse only for pleasure. Rather, his only purpose[8] in eating and drinking shall be to keep his body and limbs healthy. Therefore he shall not eat everything that the palate desires, like a dog or an ass, but he shall eat things that are useful for him, whether bitter or sweet, and he shall not eat things bad for the body, even if they are sweet to the palate.

How so? Whoever has warm flesh shall not eat meat or honey, nor drink wine. As Solomon, for example, said: "It is not good to eat much honey, etc."[9] He shall drink chicory water, even though it is bitter. Since it is impossible for a man to live except by eating and drinking, he shall eat and drink only in accordance with the directive of medicine, in order that he become healthy and remain perfect. Likewise when he has sexual intercourse, he shall do so only to keep his body healthy and to have offspring. Therefore he shall not have sexual intercourse every time he has the desire, but whenever he knows that he needs to discharge sperm in accordance with the directive of medicine, or to have offspring.

[3] If one conducts himself in accordance with the [art of] medicine and sets his heart only upon making his body and limbs perfect and strong, and upon having sons who will do his work and labor for his needs, this is not a good way. Rather, he shall set his heart upon making his body perfect and strong so that his soul will be upright to know the Lord. For it is impossible for him to understand and reflect upon wisdom[10] when he is sick or when one of his limbs is in pain. He shall set his heart upon having a son who perhaps will be a wise and great man in Israel. Whoever follows this way all his days serves the Lord continuously, even when he engages in business and even when he has sexual intercourse, because his thought in everything is to fulfill his needs so that his body will be perfect to serve the Lord.

Even when he sleeps, if he sleeps with the intention of resting his mind and his body so that he does not become sick—for he is unable to serve the Lord when he is sick—his sleep shall become a service of the Lord,[11] blessed be He. Concerning this subject, the wise men commanded, saying: "Let all your deeds be for the sake of Heaven."[12] That is what Solomon said in his wisdom: "In all your ways know Him, and He will make your paths straight."[13]

CHAPTER FOUR

[1] Since preserving the body's health and strength is among the ways of the Lord—for to attain understanding and knowledge is impossible when one is sick—a man needs to keep away from things that destroy the body and to accustom himself to things that make him healthy and vigorous. They are as follows. A man should eat only when he is hungry and drink only when he is thirsty. Whenever he needs to urinate or defecate, he should do so at once; he should not delay for even a single moment.

[2] A man should not eat until his stomach is full, but about one-fourth less than would make him sated. He should not drink water with the food, except a little mixed with wine. When the food begins to be digested in his intestines, he should drink what he needs to drink. He should not drink an excessive amount of water even when the food is being digested. He should not eat until he has examined himself very well, lest he needs to ease himself.

A man should not eat unless he first takes a walk so that his body becomes heated, or he should work or exert himself in some other way. The general rule is that he should afflict his body and exert himself every day in the morning until his body starts to become hot. Then he should rest a little until his soul is tranquil, and then eat. If he washes with warm water after his exertion, that is good. Afterward, he should wait a little and then eat.

[3] While he is eating, a man should always sit at his place or incline to the left, and should neither walk nor ride. He should not exert himself nor shake his body nor take a long walk until all the food in his intestines is digested. Anyone who takes long walks or exerts himself immediately after eating brings bad and severe illnesses upon himself.

[4] Day and night have altogether twenty-four hours. It suffices for a man to sleep one-third of them, i.e., eight hours, at the end of the night, so that there be eight hours from the beginning of his sleep until the sun rises. He should stand up from his bed before the sun rises.

[5] A man should not sleep upon his face, nor upon his back, but upon his side; at the beginning of the night, on the left side,

and at the end of the night, on the right side. He should not go to sleep shortly after eating. He should not sleep during the day.

[6] Things which loosen the bowels, such as grapes, figs, mulberries, pears, melons, and the pulp of cucumbers and gherkins, are eaten before the meal. One should not mix them with the meal, but wait a little until they leave the upper stomach, and then eat the meal. Things which harden the bowels, such as pomegranates, quinces, apples, and small pears, are eaten immediately after the meal, and not in excess.

[7] When a man wants to eat poultry and the meat of cattle together, he should first eat the poultry. In the case of eggs and poultry, he should first eat the eggs. In the case of the meat of lean cattle and of heavy cattle, he should first eat the meat of the lean cattle. He should always have light food before heavy food.

[8] In hot weather he should eat cold foods, without much condiment, and sour food. In the rainy season[1] he should eat warm foods, with a lot of condiment, and a little mustard and asafetida. He should do so in cold as well as hot places, in accordance with what is appropriate for each place.

[9] There are foods that are exceedingly bad and it is never proper for a man to eat them, such as large, salted, stale fish; salted, stale cheese; truffles and mushrooms; salted, stale meat; wine from the press; cooked food kept until its odor disappears; and likewise every food whose odor is bad or exceedingly bitter—these are like poison for the body.

There are foods that are bad, but not as bad as the above. Consequently, it is proper for a man to eat only a little of them, at long intervals, and not to accustom himself to make a meal of them or continually to eat them with his food. For example: large fish, cheese, milk kept twenty-four hours after milking, meat of large oxen and large goats, beans, lentils, chickpeas, barley bread, unleavened bread, cabbage, leeks, onions, garlic, mustard, and radishes. All these are bad foods.

It is proper for a man to eat only very little of them and then only in the rainy season; he should not eat them at all outside of the rainy season. It is not proper to eat beans and lentils in either hot weather or the rainy season. Gourds may be eaten a little in hot weather.

[10] There are foods that are bad, but not as bad as the above. They are: water fowl, young pigeons, dates, meat juice, fish brine, and bread baked in oil or kneaded in oil and fine flour sifted to such an extent that no trace of coarse bran remains. It is not proper to eat much of these foods. A man who is wise and conquers his impulse does not succumb to his desire to eat from any of the above-mentioned at all, except if he has need of them for medicine. He is indeed a powerful man.[2]

[11] A man should always restrain himself from eating the fruit of trees. He should not eat much of them even when they are dried and, needless to say, when they are fresh.[3] For before they are cooked sufficiently, they are like daggers to the body, Likewise carob-pods are always bad. All sour fruit is bad and should not be eaten, except for a little in hot weather or in hot places. Figs, grapes, and almonds are always good, whether fresh or dried, and a man may eat of them whatever he needs. But he should not eat them continually, even though they are the best of all the fruit from trees. [12] Honey and wine are bad for children, but fine for old people, especially in the rainy season. In hot weather, a man needs to eat two-thirds of what he eats in the rainy season.

[13] All his days a man should try always to keep his bowels loose and be a bit close to diarrhea. This is an important general rule in medicine, for whenever the stool is blocked or expelled with difficulty, many illnesses result.

What should he loosen his bowels with if they are a little firm? If he is a youth, he should eat salted, boiled food, seasoned with oil, fish brine, and salt, and not eat bread; or he should drink the juice of boiled spinach or cabbage, with oil, salt, and fish brine. If he is old, he should drink honey mixed with warm water in the morning, and wait about four hours, after which he should eat his meal. He should do so day after day, for three or four days if necessary, until his bowels are loosened.

[14] Still another general rule: they said about the health of the body that if a man does much exercise and hard work and is not sated and his bowels are loose, he will not become sick and his strength will increase, even if he eats bad food. [15] Whoever leads a sedentary life and does not exercise, or delays

excretion or has hard bowels, even if he eats good food and guards himself in accordance with medical practice, all his days will be painful and his strength will diminish. Gross eating is like deadly poison for the body of any man; it is a root of all illness.

Most of the illnesses that come to a man are due either to bad foods or to stuffing the stomach. Solomon, in his wisdom, says about the one who eats in a gross manner (even though the food is good): "He who guards his mouth and his tongue guards his soul from troubles."[4] That is to say, he guards his mouth from eating bad food or from being sated, and his tongue from speaking, except in connection with his needs.

[16] The way to bathe is to enter the bath every seven days, and not enter shortly before eating or when hungry, but when the food begins to be digested. A man should wash his whole body with water that is not so hot that the body would be burned by it, but wash only his head with water so hot it would burn the body. Afterward he should wash his body with lukewarm water, and after that with water even less warm, until he washes with cold water. He should not let any lukewarm or cold water pass over his head. He should not wash with cold water in the rainy season, nor wash until his whole body perspires and becomes pliant, nor remain long in the bath, but when he perspires and his body becomes pliant he should rinse and leave.

He should test himself before he enters the bath and after he leaves, lest he needs to ease himself; likewise a man should inspect himself before and after eating, before and after sexual intercourse, before and after he exerts himself with exercise, before he goes to sleep and after he awakens—ten times in all.

[17] When a man leaves the bath, he should put on his clothes and cover his head in the anteroom, so that a cold breeze does not overcome him. Even in hot weather, he needs to be careful and pause after he leaves the bath until his soul is tranquil, his body is at rest, and he is no longer warm. Afterward he should eat, and if he sleeps a little when he leaves the bath before eating, that is indeed very fine. A man should not drink cold water when he leaves the bath and, needless to say, he should not drink in the bath. If he is thirsty when he

leaves the bath and is unable to restrain himself, he should mix water with wine or honey and drink it. During the rainy season if he has a massage with oil at the bath after he rinses, that is good.

[18] A man should not accustom himself to have blood let continually; he should not have blood let unless there is an extraordinary need. He should not have blood let in either hot weather or the rainy season, except during the month of Nissan and a little during the month of Tishri. After age fifty, he should not have blood let at all. A man should not have blood let and enter the bath on the same day. He should not have blood let when he sets out on a trip, nor when he returns from a trip. On the day of bloodletting, he should eat and drink less than what he is accustomed to; he should rest and neither exercise nor take a long walk.

[19] Semen is the strength of the body and its life, and is the light of the eyes. Whenever too much is ejaculated, the body decays, its strength is spent, and its life destroyed. As Solomon said in his wisdom: "Do not give your strength to women, and your years to that which destroys kings."[5]

As for anyone who overindulges in sexual intercourse: old age pounces upon him; his strength fails; his eyes become dim; a bad odor spreads from his mouth and armpits; the hair on his head, his eyebrows, and his eyelashes fall out; the hair of his beard, armpits, and legs grows excessively; his teeth fall out; and many pains in addition to these come to him.

The wise men among the physicians said: one in a thousand dies from other illnesses, and the rest from excessive copulation. Therefore a man needs to be careful in this matter if he wishes to live well. He should only have sexual intercourse when his body is healthy and exceedingly strong and he has a continuous, involuntary erection and he distracts himself with something else, but the erection remains as it was, and he finds a heaviness in his loins and below, as if the cords of the testicles were drawn out, and his flesh is hot. Such a man needs to have sexual intercourse and his medicine is to have sexual intercourse.

A man should not have sexual intercourse when he is sated or hungry, but after the food is digested in his intestines. Before and after sexual intercourse, he should test[6] to see whether he needs to ease himself. He should not have sexual intercourse in either a standing or sitting position, nor in the bathhouse, nor on the day he enters the bath, nor on the day of bloodletting, nor on the day of departure or return from a trip —neither before nor afterward.

[20] Whoever conducts himself along the paths we have taught, I guarantee will not become ill all his days, until he is very old and dies. He will not need a physician and his body will be perfect and remain healthy all his days, unless it is defective from the beginning of its creation, or he has become accustomed to a bad habit from the time of birth, or a pestilence or drought comes to the world.

[21] It is only proper for a healthy man to adhere to these good habits about which we have spoken. But as for a sick man, or one with a sick organ, or one who is accustomed to a bad habit for many years—for each of them there are other paths and practices, depending upon his illness, as is explained in the medical books. "A change of custom is the beginning of illness."[7]

[22] Whether a man is healthy or sick, if he lives in a place where there is no physician, it is not proper for him to depart from any of the paths we have discussed in this chapter, for every one of them results in some good.

[23] A disciple of wise men[8] is not permitted to live in any city that does not have these ten things: a physician, a surgeon, a bathhouse, a bathroom, a fixed source of water such as a river or spring, a synagogue, a teacher of children, a scribe, a collector of charity, and a court that can punish with lashes and imprisonment.[9].

CHAPTER FIVE

[1] The wise man is identified by his wisdom and his character traits, which distinguish him from the rest of the people. Similarly, he needs to be identified by his actions: by his eating, his drinking, his sexual intercourse, his relieving himself, his speech, his walking, his dress, the management of his affairs, and his business conduct. All of these actions are to be exceptionally decent and fitting.

How so? A disciple of wise men shall not be a glutton, but eat food that is suitable for making the body healthy. He shall not eat in a gross manner, nor run to fill his stomach, like those who stuff themselves with food and drink until their belly swells. The tradition applies the following verse to such people: "And I will spread dung on your faces, even the dung of your holiday sacrifices (*haggeikhem*)."[1] The wise men said: "These are the people who eat and drink and make all their days like holidays (*haggim*)."[2]

They are the same people who say: "Eat and drink for tomorrow we die."[3] This is how the wicked eat, whose tables Scripture censured by saying: "For all tables are full of filthy vomit, and no place is clean."[4]

However, the wise man only eats one or two courses, eating from them what suffices for life, which is enough for him. That is what Solomon said: "A just man eats to satisfy his desire."[5]

[2] When the wise man eats the little that is suitable for him, he shall eat it only in his house, at his table. He shall not eat in a store nor in the marketplace, except in case of great need, so that he is not degraded before his fellow creatures. He shall not eat with ignoramuses nor at those tables full of "filthy vomit." He shall not frequent feasts at a variety of places, even with the wise men. He shall not eat at feasts where there is a large gathering. It is not proper for him to eat at a feast unless it involves fulfilling a commandment, such as a feast of betrothal or marriage, and then only if a disciple of wise men marries the daughter of a disciple of wise men. The just men and[6] the pious men of old[7] never ate at a feast not their own.

[3] When the wise man drinks wine, he drinks only in order to loosen the food in his intestines. Anyone who becomes drunk commits a sin, is contemptible, and loses his wisdom. If he becomes drunk before ignoramuses, he profanes the Name. It is forbidden to drink at noon, even a little, unless it is part of the meal, for drinking which is part of the meal does not make one drunk. They [the wise men] warn only about wine that comes after the meal.

[4] Even though a man's wife is always permitted to him, it is proper for a disciple of wise men to conduct himself in holiness and not be with his wife like a rooster, but [be with her] only on the night of the Sabbath, if he has the strength. When he cohabits with her, he shall not cohabit at the beginning of the night when he is sated, nor at the end of the night when he is

hungry, but in the middle of the night when the food in his intestines is digested.

He shall not be frivolous, nor dirty his mouth with obscenity,[8] even between himself and her. Indeed, it says in the tradition: "He [God] tells a man what his conversation was."[9] The wise men said: "Judgment is made in the future even upon a frivolous conversation between a man and his wife."[10]

Both of them (or one of them) shall not be drunk, lethargic, or sad. She should not be asleep and he should not force her if she is unwilling, but [intercourse shall take place] when both wish it and in state of mutual joy. He shall converse and play with her a little so that their souls become tranquil, and he shall have sexual intercourse modestly, not shamelessly, and separate [from her] at once.

[5] Anyone accustomed to this conduct not only makes his soul holy, purifies himself, and improves his character traits, but also, if he has sons, they will be decent and modest,[11] fit for wisdom and piety. Anyone accustomed to the conduct of the rest of the people, who walk in darkness, will have sons like those people.

[6] Disciples of wise men are accustomed to behave with great modesty.[12] They do not degrade themselves; they uncover neither their heads nor their bodies. Even after entering the toilet, one must be modest and not uncover his garments until he sits down. He shall not wipe with the right hand. He shall move away from everyone and [for example] enter the innermost room of a cave and relieve himself there. If he relieves himself behind a fence, he shall go far away so that his fellow man will not hear a sound if he breaks wind. If he relieves himself in a plain, he shall go far away so that his fellow man will not see him uncovered. He shall not speak when he relieves himself, even in case of great need. He conducts himself with the same modesty in the toilet at night as by day. A man shall forever train himself to relieve himself only in the morning and the evening, so that he does not have to go off at a distance.

[7] A disciple of wise men shall not shout and scream when he speaks, like cattle and wild beasts. He shall not raise his voice much, but speak calmly with all his fellow creatures. When he speaks calmly, he shall be careful not to be aloof, lest his words appear to be like the words of the arrogant. He greets every

man first,[13] so that they will be pleasantly disposed toward him. He judges every man in a favorable light.[14] He speaks in praise of his fellow man, never disparagingly. He loves peace and seeks peace.[15]

If he sees a place where his words would be useful and listened to, he speaks and, if not, he remains silent. How so? He does not appease his friend in the hour of his anger; he does not ask about his vow at the time he makes the vow, but waits until his mind becomes cool and is calm; he does not comfort [his friend] while his dead lie before him because he is in a state of shock until the burial;[16] and so too, in all similar circumstances. He does not appear before his friend in the hour of his disgrace, but hides his eyes from him.[17]

He shall not alter what he says; he shall neither add nor detract, except in matters concerning peace and the like. The general rule is that he speaks only in performing deeds of loving-kindness or about matters of wisdom and the like. He shall not converse with a woman in the marketplace, even if she is his wife, sister, or daughter.[18]

[8] A disciple of wise men shall not walk with an erect carriage[19] and outstretched neck. As it is said: "And they walk with outstretched necks and wanton eyes."[20] He shall not walk mincingly and smugly, like the women and the arrogant about whom it is said: "Walking and tripping along, making a tinkling sound with their feet."[21]

He shall not run in a public place and behave in a crazy manner, nor bend over like hunchbacks. Rather he looks down, like someone praying, and walks straight ahead, like a man preoccupied with his affairs.

In his manner of walking, too, a man is recognized as wise and sensible,[22] or else a simpleton and a fool. Thus, Solomon said in his wisdom: "Also in the way the fool walks he lacks thought, and he says to everyone that he is a fool."[23] He announces about himself to all that he is a fool.

[9] The dress of a disciple of wise men is becoming[24] and clean. It is forbidden for a stain, a fatty spot, and the like to be found on his garment. He shall not wear the dress of the poor, which degrades those who wear it, but garments that are becoming[24] and in the middle [way].

His flesh must not show from beneath his clothing, as

happens with the exceedingly light, linen garments that they make in Egypt, nor shall his garments drag on the earth, as do the garments of the arrogant, but they shall extend down to his heel and his sleeve extend down to his fingertips. He shall not let his garment hang down because he would appear like the arrogant, except on the Sabbath, if he has no change of clothing. In hot weather he shall not wear patched shoes and a garment with patch over patch, but in the rainy season this is permitted if he is poor.

He shall not go perfumed to the marketplace, with perfumed garments or with perfume on his hair, but if his skin is massaged with perfume to remove a foul smell, it is permitted. So too, he shall not go out alone at night, unless he has a set time to go out in order to study. All these [laws] are to avoid suspicion.[25]

[10] A disciple of wise men conducts his affairs judiciously. His eating and drinking and his support of the members of his household depend upon his income and his success. He shall not burden himself excessively. The wise men commanded concerning the proper regimen that a man eat meat only when he has the desire.[26] As it is said: "Because your soul desires to eat meat."[27] It is enough for a healthy man to eat meat on the eve of the Sabbath. If he is rich enough to eat meat every day, he may do so.

The wise men commanded, saying: "A man shall always eat less than is suitable for him according to his income, dress as is suitable for him, and honor his wife and children more than is suitable for him."[28]

[11] A sensible man[29] first establishes himself in an occupation which supports him, afterward he buys a home, and after that he marries a woman. As it is said: "What man is there who has planted a vineyard and has not used the fruit thereof; who has built a new house and has not dedicated it; who is betrothed to a woman and has not taken her?"[30] But the fool begins by marrying a woman after which, if he can, he buys a house and, after that, at the end of his days, he finally seeks a trade or he is supported by charity. Thus it says in the [enumeration of] curses: "A woman shall you betroth . . . a house shall you build . . . a vineyard shall you plant."[31] That is to say, your deeds shall be the reverse [of what is proper], so that you shall

not make your paths prosper. In the blessing, what does it say? "And David had success in all his paths, and the Lord was with him."[32]

[12] A man is forbidden to renounce ownership of all his possessions and to dedicate them to the Temple, and then to become a burden upon his fellow creatures. He shall not sell a field and buy a house, nor sell a house and then either buy movable goods or do business with the funds from his house, but he may sell movable goods and buy a field. The general rule is that he set his goal to improve his possessions, not to have a little pleasure for the moment, or to have a little pleasure and then suffer a great loss.

[13] The business conduct of the disciples of wise men is truthful and faithful. His "no" is no and his "yes" yes. He is scrupulous with himself in his reckoning. He gives in and yields to others when he buys from them and is not exacting of them. He gives the sale-price on the spot. He does not allow himself to be made a surety or a guarantor and does not accept the power of attorney. He obligates himself in matters of buying and selling in circumstances where the Torah does not obligate him, so that he stands by his word and does not change it.[33] If others are obligated to him by law, he gives them time and is forgiving. He lends money and is gracious. He shall not take away business from his fellow man[34] nor bring grief to any man in the world during his lifetime.

The general rule is that he be among the oppressed and not the oppressors, among the insulted and not those who insult.[35] Scripture says about a man who performs all these actions and their like: "And He said to me, 'You are My servant Israel, in whom I will be glorified.' "[36]

CHAPTER SIX

[1] Man is created in such a way that his character traits and actions are influenced by his neighbors and friends, and he follows the custom of the people in his city. Therefore a man needs to associate with the just and be with the wise continually in order to learn [from] their actions, and to keep away from the wicked, who walk in darkness, so that he avoids learning from their actions. That is what Solomon said: "He who walks

with wise men will become wise, but he who associates with fools will become evil."[1] And it says: "Blessed is the man who does not walk in the council of the wicked, etc."[2] Likewise, if he is in a city with evil customs where men do not follow the right way, he shall go to a place where men are just and they follow the way of good men. If all the cities he knows or hears about follow a way that is not good, as in our time, or if because of military conscription or illness, he is unable to go to a city with good customs, he shall dwell alone in solitude. As it is said: "Let him dwell alone and be silent."[3] If there are evil men and sinners who do not let him live in the city unless he mingles with them and follows their evil customs, he shall go off to the caves, the briers, or the desert, and not accustom himself to the way of sinners. As it is said: "O that I were in the desert, in a lodging place of wayfaring men."[4]

[2] It is a positive commandment to cleave to the wise men in order to learn from their actions. As it is said: "And to Him shall you cleave."[5] Is it possible for a man to cleave to the *Shekhinah* [Presence]? But thus said the wise men in explaining this commandment: cleave to the wise men and their disciples.[6] Therefore a man needs to try to marry the daughter of a disciple of wise men; to give his daughter in marriage to a disciple of wise men; to eat and drink with the disciples of wise men; to do business on behalf of the disciples of wise men; and to associate with them in all kinds of associations. As it is said: "And cleave to Him."[7] Thus the wise men commanded, saying: "Sit in the dust of their feet and drink in thirst their words."[8]

[3] It is a commandment for every man to love every single individual of Israel like his own body. As it is said: "And you shall love your neighbor as yourself."[9] Therefore he needs to speak in praise of him and to have concern for his possessions, just as he has concern for his own possessions and wants to be honored himself. Whoever glorifies himself through the humiliation of his fellow man has no portion in the world-to-come.[10]

[4] There are two positive commandments to love the convert[11] who comes under the wings of the *Shekhinah*; one, because he is in the class of neighbors, and the other, because he is a convert and the Torah said: "And you shall love the stranger."[12] He [God] commanded the love of the convert, just as He commanded the love of His Name. As it is said: "And you

shall love the Lord your God."[13] The Holy One Himself, blessed be He, loves the converts. As it is said: "And He loves the stranger."[14]

[5] Anyone who hates one Israelite in his heart transgresses a prohibition. As it is said: "You shall not hate your brother in your heart."[15] They do not give lashes in connection with this prohibition, since it does not refer to an action. The Torah warned [here] only about hatred in the heart, but whoever strikes his fellow man and reviles him, even though it is not permitted, does not transgress what is prohibited by the verse, "You shall not hate. . . ."

[6] When a man sins against another man, he [the latter] shall not hate him and remain silent. As it is said about the wicked: "And Absalom spoke to Amnon neither good nor evil, although Absalom hated Amnon."[16] Rather, he is commanded to speak to him, and to say to him: "Why did you do such-and-such to me? Why did you sin against me in such-and-such a matter?" As it is said: "You shall surely rebuke your neighbor."[17] If he repents and requests forgiveness from him, he needs to forgive and shall not be cruel. As it is said: "And Abraham prayed to God, etc."[18]

[7] If someone sees his fellow man who has sinned or who follows a way that is not good, it is a commandment to make him return to the good and to make known to him that he sins against himself by his evil actions. As it is said: "You shall surely rebuke your neighbor."[19]

Whoever rebukes his fellow man, whether concerning matters between the two of them or between him [the fellow man] and God,[20] needs to rebuke him in private. He shall speak to him calmly and gently, and make known to him that he talks to him only for his own good, to bring him to the life of the world-to-come. If he accepts it from him, good; if not, he shall rebuke him a second and a third time. Thus he is always obliged to rebuke him until the sinner strikes him and says to him, "I will not listen."[21] If he does not prevent everything he can possibly prevent, he is ensnared in the sin of all those he could have prevented from sinning.

[8] Whoever rebukes his fellow man shall not at first speak harshly so as to put him to shame. As it is said: "You shall not bear sin on his account."[22] Thus said the wise men: "Are we to

assume he should rebuke him until his face changes [its expression or color]? The text therefore says: 'You shall not bear sin on his account.' "[23] From this we learn it is forbidden to humiliate an Israelite; all the more [is it forbidden] in public.

Even though the one who humiliates his fellow man is not given lashes, it is a great sin. Thus said the wise men: "Whoever puts his fellow man to shame in public has no portion in the world-to-come."[24]

Therefore a man needs to be careful that he not shame his fellow man—be he young or old—in public, nor call him by a name he is ashamed of, nor speak about something in front of him that would make him ashamed.

To what matters does the above refer? To matters between a man and his fellow man, but in matters of Heaven if he does not repent in private, he is to be humiliated in public, his sin is proclaimed, and he is reviled to his face and degraded and cursed until he returns to the good. That is what all the prophets did with Israel.

[9] If someone is sinned against by his fellow man and does not wish to rebuke him or to say anything to him—because the sinner is exceedingly simple or his mind is distraught—and if he forgives him in his heart and bears no animosity toward him and does not rebuke him, this is indeed the measure of piety. The Torah was particularly concerned only about animosity.

[10] A man is obliged to be careful about widows and orphans because their souls are very lowly and their spirits submissive, even if they are wealthy. We are even warned about the widow and the orphans of a king. As it is said: "You shall not afflict any widow or orphan."[25]

How should we conduct ourselves toward them? A man shall speak only softly to them, treat them only with honor, and not afflict their bodies with labor nor their hearts with words. He shall have more concern for their possessions than for his own. If anyone belittles them, vexes them, afflicts their hearts, subjugates them, or loses their money, he transgresses a prohibition, and all the more if he strikes or curses them. Although lashes are not given in such cases, the punishment is expressly stated in the Torah: "My wrath shall wax hot, and I will slay you with the sword."[26]

A covenant was made for them by Him who spoke and the

world came to be. Whenever they cry out because of violence, they are answered. As it is said: "For if they cry out at all to Me, I will surely hear their cry."²⁷ To what do these words refer? To a man's afflicting them for his own needs, but if a teacher afflicts them in order to teach them Torah or a craft or to guide them on the right way,²⁸ this is indeed permitted. Nevertheless, he shall not treat them the way he is accustomed to treat every man, but shall make a distinction and guide them calmly, with great mercy and honor—"For the Lord will plead their cause"²⁹ —whether the orphan has lost his father or mother. For how long are they called orphans with respect to this matter? Until they have no need of an adult to depend upon for their nurture and their care, but the orphan can fulfill all his own needs like any other adult.

CHAPTER SEVEN

[1] Whoever speaks ill of his fellow man transgresses a prohibition. As it is said: "You shall not go about as a talebearer among My people."¹ Even though they do not give lashes in connection with this prohibition, it is a great sin and causes many people of Israel to be killed. Therefore it is followed by the verse: "And you shall not stand idly by the blood of your neighbor."² Go and learn what happened in the case of Doeg the Edomite.³

[2] Who is a talebearer? He who carries words and goes from one person to another, saying: "A certain individual said such-and-such"; "I heard such-and-such about a certain individual." Even though he speaks the truth, this man destroys the world.

There is a far greater sin that falls under this prohibition. It is "the evil tongue," which refers to whoever speaks disparagingly of his fellow man, even though he speaks the truth. But whoever tells a lie is called, "one who gives his fellow man a bad name." However, the one who possesses an "evil tongue" sits and says: "A certain individual did such-and-such"; "his ancestors were so-and-so"; "I heard such-and-such about him." Scripture says concerning whoever speaks disparagingly about someone: "May the Lord cut off all smooth lips, the tongue that speaks proud things."⁴

[3] The wise men said: "For three transgressions punish-

ment is exacted from a man in this world and he has no portion in the world-to-come: idol worship, illicit sexual unions, and the shedding of blood. And the evil tongue is equal to all of them put together."[5] Moreover, the wise men said: "Whoever speaks with an evil tongue [behaves] as if he denied God.[6] As it is said: 'They said, "With our tongues we will prevail, our lips are with us. Who is lord over us?" ' "[7] Furthermore, the wise men said: "The evil tongue slays three: the one who speaks, the one who accepts it, and the one who is spoken about; the one who accepts it more so than the one who speaks."[8]

[4] There are also words that are "dust of the evil tongue." For example: "Who would have thought that so-and-so would become like he is now?" Or someone says: "Be still about so-and-so; I do not wish to tell about what happened and what took place." And words like these. So too, the one who speaks well of someone before his enemies; this too is "dust of the evil tongue," for that would cause them to speak disparagingly of him. Concerning this matter, Solomon said: "He who blesses his neighbor with a loud voice, rising early in the morning, will be regarded as cursing."[9] For out of the good [said] of him comes evil.

It is also [dust of the evil tongue] if one speaks with an evil tongue in jest and levity, that is, speaks without hatred. This is what Solomon says: "Like a madman who throws firebrands, arrows, and death is the man who deceives his neighbor and says, 'I am only jesting.' "[10] And, so too, if one speaks with an evil tongue deceitfully, feigning innocence, as though he does not know that it is evil speech.[11] When they protest about it, he says: "I did not know that these are the deeds of so-and-so or that this is evil speech."[11]

[5] It is all the same whether he speaks with an evil tongue in the presence of his fellow man or not in his presence. Whoever relates things which, if repeated, would harm the body or possessions of his fellow man, or would only distress or frighten him—this is the evil tongue! If these words are spoken in the presence of three people, the matter is regarded as public knowledge. If one of the three relates it once again, it is not classified as the evil tongue, assuming that he does not intend to make a proclamation and to be excessive in the disclosure.

[6] It is forbidden to dwell in the vicinity of any of those with

an evil tongue, and all the more to sit with them and to listen to their words. The judgment against our fathers in the desert was decreed solely because of the evil tongue.[12]

[7] One who takes vengeance against his fellow man transgresses a prohibition. As it is said: "You shall not take vengeance."[13] Even though he is not given lashes, this is an extremely bad character trait.[14] It is proper for a man to overlook all the things of the world, for according to those who understand, everything is vain and empty and not worth taking vengeance for.

What is vengeance? His friend says: "Lend me your axe." He says: "I will not lend it to you." The next day, [the other] needs to borrow from him and says: "Lend me your axe." He says: "I will not lend it to you, for you did not lend your axe to me when I asked you for it." This is taking vengeance.[15] Rather, when someone comes to him to borrow, he shall give with a perfect heart and not repay in kind. So too, with all things like these. So too, David said, referring to his good character traits: "If I have repaid my friend with evil or plundered my enemy without cause, etc."[16]

[8] Likewise, whoever bears a grudge against any Israelite transgresses a prohibition. As it is said: "You shall not bear a grudge against the sons of your people."[17] How so? Reuben said to Simon: "Rent this house to me" or "Lend this ox to me." Simon did not wish to. After several days, Simon needed to borrow from Reuben or to rent from him. Reuben said to him: "Here you are, I will lend it to you. I am not like you. I will not pay you back in kind." The one who acts like this transgresses the verse: "You shall not bear a grudge."[18]

Rather, he shall blot out the matter from his heart and not bear a grudge. If he bears a grudge over something[19] and remembers it, he might come to take vengeance. Therefore the Torah was particularly concerned with grudge-bearing so that the wrong done be completely blotted out from a man's heart and he not remember it. This is the appropriate character trait; it makes possible the settlement of the earth and social relations[20] among human beings.[21]

Blessed be the Merciful One
who has helped us.

NOTES

CHAPTER ONE

1. These commandments are all based upon verses from Scripture cited in the main body of the text.
2. The text has the pural: *benei 'adam.*
3. The primary meaning of this word is "soul."
4. Eccles. 5:9.
5. See *infra, Guide,* II 40, for the significance of introducing the commandment concerning the mean with a description of character traits at the two extremes.
6. I.e., conception. Cf. *H. De'ot,* IV 20, where the beginning of a man's creation is contrasted with the time of his birth.
7. Or: straight path.
8. Literally: a middle measure.
9. Literally: the first wise men.
10. Cf. *Babylonian Talmud* (cited henceforth as *B.T.*), Mo'ed Qatan, 5a; Sotah, 5b.
11. Prov. 13:25. The last word in this verse could also be translated as "soul."
12. Ps. 37:16.
13. Literally: the first pious men.
14. A rabbinic expression for going beyond what is required by the Law.
15. Or: straight.
16. Deut. 28:9.
17. According to *B.T.*, Shabbat, 133b, just as God is gracious and merciful, man must be gracious and merciful. Cf. *Sifre* to Deut. 10:12, which teaches that just as God is merciful, gracious, just, and pious (*hasid*), so too, man must acquire these qualities. The command to imitate the holiness of God is based on Lev. 19:2.
18. *Yashar,* translated above as "right."
19. Or: straight (*yashar*).
20. The traditional version reads: "to imitate Him." The last word is omitted in the Hyamson edition.
21. *Yotzer.*
22. Gen. 18:19.
23. *Ibid.*

CHAPTER TWO

1. Isa. 5:20.
2. Prov. 2:13.
3. Prov. 1:7.
4. Literally: middle measure.
5. Literally: low.
6. Num. 12:3.
7. *Mishnah,* Avot, IV 4.
8. Literally: the root.
9. *B.T.,* Sotah, 4b; Deut. 8:14.
10. *B.T.,* Sotah, 5a.
11. Literally: the first wise men.
12. Cf. *B.T.,* Shabbat, 115b.
13. *B.T.,* Pesahim, 66b.
14. *Ibid.,* 113b.
15. *B.T.,* Yoma, 23a; Gittin 36b.
16. Cf. *B.T.,* Sukkah, 28a, where this is reported about R. Yohanan ben Zakkai. "Our holy master" refers to R. Judah the Prince.
17. *Mishnah,* Avot, I 16.
18. *Ibid.* Maimonides interprets the word *guf* in the rabbinic passage quite literally as "body." It might also mean something like "principle," in which case the passage would read: "I have found no better principle than silence."
19. *B.T.,* Pesahim, 3b.
20. Eccles. 5:2.
21. *Mishnah,* Avot, III 16.
22. Eccles. 9:17.
23. Literally: steal the opinion of.
24. *Mishnah,* Avot, III 16.
25. Cf. *ibid.*
26. The primary meaning of this word is "soul."
27. Literally: possess a good eye. This refers to the virtue of contentment, according to Maimonides' Commentary on *Avot,* II 12.
28. *Mishnah,* Avot, IV 12.
29. Cf. *ibid.,* IV 1.
30. *Ibid.,* IV 27.
31. Literally: the middle measure.
32. Prov. 4:26. The full verse reads: "Balance the course of your steps, and all your ways will be upright."

CHAPTER THREE

1. *Na'eh,* which can have the connotation of being suitable, attractive, or becoming. Cf. *C.M.,* Eight Chapters, V (*infra,* p. 77), where *na'eh* is translated as "attractive."

2. I.e., Christian monks.
3. Num. 6:11.
4. *B.T.*, Ta'anit 11a; Nedarim, 10a; Nazir, 19a, 22a; Baba Qamma, 91b.
5. *Jerusalem Talmud*, Nedarim, IX 1.
6. Eccles. 7:16.
7. Maimonides is emphatic here. Literally: the man (*ha-'adam*).
8. Literally: he shall place upon his heart. According to the Jewish tradition, the heart is the location of both thought and will.
9. Prov. 25:27.
10. The text has the plural and (presumably) the definite article: the wisdoms.
11. Literally: the Place (a talmudic term for God).
12. *Mishnah*, Avot, II 15.
13. Prov. 3:6.

CHAPTER FOUR

1. The rainy season refers to the winter months.
2. Cf. *Mishnah*, Avot, IV 1: "Who is a powerful man (*gibbor*)? He who conquers his impulse."
3. Literally: wet.
4. Prov. 21:23.
5. Prov. 31:3. The biblical verse reads, "your ways"; the edition of Hyamson reads, "your years."
6. Reading *yivdoq* with the traditional version and the Constantinople edition; Hyamson has *yivdo*.
7. *B.T.*, Baba Batra, 146a; Ketuvot, 110b.
8. *Talmid ha-hakhamim*, which refers to an advanced student of the Law, who might even be elderly.
9. *B.T.*, Sanhedrin, 17b. The passage there reads: "A disciple of a wise man [or a wise disciple] is not permitted to live in a city that does not have these ten things: a court that can give lashes and exact penalities, charity collected by two [men] and distributed by three, a synagogue, a bathhouse, a bathroom, a physician, a surgeon, a scribe, a butcher, and a teacher of children."

CHAPTER FIVE

1. Malachi 2:3.
2. *B.T.*, Shabbat, 151b. The passage there reads: "These are the people who forsake the words of Torah and make all their days like holidays."
3. Isa. 22:13.

4. Isa. 28:8.
5. Prov. 13:25. The last word in this verse could also be translated as "soul."
6. Reading with the traditional version, the Rome edition, the Constantinople edition, and many manuscripts cited in Lieberman; Hyamson has "the pious, just men of old."
7. Literally: the first pious men.
8. Literally: words of vanity (or exaggeration).
9. Amos 4:13.
10. *B.T.*, Hagigah, 5b.
11. Or: have a sense of shame (*bayyshanin*).
12. *Seniy'ut*, as distinct from *bushah*, which is found at the end of V 4. *Bushah* can have the connotation of a "sense of shame."
13. *Mishnah*, Avot, IV 20.
14. *Ibid.*, I 6. More literally: he inclines toward judging every man as being on the scale of merit.
15. *Ibid.*, I 12.
16. *Ibid.*, IV 23.
17. *Ibid.*
18. *B.T.*, Berakhot, 43b.
19. *B.T.*, Kiddushin, 31a. Cf. *Guide*, III 52.
20. Isa. 3:16.
21. *Ibid.*
22. *Ba'al de'ah*. Literally: a master of intellect, or of character trait.
23. Eccles. 10:3.
24. See *supra*, Chapter Three, note one.
25. *B.T.*, Berakhot, 43b. If he is perfumed, he might be suspected of being a homosexual. If he is not accustomed to go out alone at night, he might be suspected of some other improper conduct.
26. *B.T.*, Hullin, 84a.
27. Deut. 12:20.
28. *B.T.*, Hullin, 84b.
29. The text has the plural (*ba'alei de'ah*). Cf. note twenty-two.
30. Cf. Deut. 20:6,5,7. Maimonides changes the order found in the Bible.
31. Deut. 28:30. The complete verse reads: "A woman shall you betroth and another man shall lie with her; a house shall you build and you shall not dwell in it; a vineyard shall you plant and not use the fruit thereof."
32. I Sam. 18:14.
33. According to Jewish law, "a purchase is not made with words." The sale must be consummated by the payment of money, signing a contract, or some other legally binding method (*M.T.*, Laws of Selling, I). The disciples of the wise go beyond what the Law requires.
34. Or: his friend. The word *haver*, usually translated as "fellow man," does not have universalistic overtones. It means "friend," "associate," "fellow."

35. Cf. *supra,* II 3, p. 32.
36. Isa. 49:3. This verse is also quoted at the end of the fifth chapter in *M.T.,* Laws of the Foundation of the Torah. That chapter deals with the sanctification of God's name and ends with an exhortation to wise men to be scrupulous in all their conduct.

CHAPTER SIX

1. Prov. 13:20.
2. Ps. 1:1.
3. Lam. 3:28.
4. Jer. 9:1.
5. Deut. 10:20.
6. *Sifre* to Deut. 10:12.
7. Deut. 11:22; *B.T.,* Ketuvot, 111b.
8. *Mishnah,* Avot, I 4.
9. Lev. 19:18.
10. *Jerusalem Talmud,* Hagigah, II 1.
11. *Ger,* which also means "stranger." Maimonides interprets the commandment, "To love the stranger," as requiring a love of the convert. Cf. *Sifra* to Lev. 19:33–34.
12. Deut. 10:19. This is the conventional translation of the verse. According to the interpretation of Maimonides, it means: "And you shall love the convert."
13. Deut. 6:5.
14. Deut. 10:18. This is the conventional translation of the verse. According to the interpretation of Maimonides, it means: "And He loves the convert."
15. Lev. 19:17.
16. II Sam. 13:22. After Amnon had forced their sister, Tamar, to lie with him, Absalom hated Amnon and did not rebuke him.
17. Lev. 19:17.
18. Gen. 20:17. After Abimelech showed regret for having taken Sarah, whom he had supposed to be Abraham's sister, Abraham asked God not to punish Abimelech.
19. Lev. 19:17.
20. Literally: the Place (a talmudic term for God).
21. *B.T.,* 'Arakhin, 16b.
22. Lev. 19:17.
23. *B.T.,* 'Arakhin, 16b.
24. *Mishnah,* Avot, III 14.
25. Exod. 22:21.
26. Exod. 22:23.
27. Exod. 22:22.
28. Or: straight path.
29. Prov. 22:23.

CHAPTER SEVEN

1. Lev. 19:16.
2. *Ibid.*
3. When Saul was in pursuit of David, Doeg the Edomite reported to Saul that David had been aided by the priest, Ahimelech of Nob. As a result, Saul had eighty-five priests of Nob put to death by the hand of Doeg. All the inhabitants of Nob were also exterminated by Doeg. I Sam. 22:6–19.
4. Ps. 12:4.
5. Cf. *B.T.*, 'Arakhin, 15b.
6. Literally: the root.
7. *B.T.*, 'Arakhin, 15b; Ps. 12:5.
8. Cf. *Jerusalem Talmud*, Pe'ah, I 1; *B.T.*, 'Arakhin, 15b.
9. Prov. 27:14.
10. Prov. 26:18–19.
11. Literally: the evil tongue.
12. *B.T.*, 'Arakhin, 15a. According to the *Talmud*, the Hebrews were not permitted to enter the promised land because they accepted the evil report of the spies concerning the land of Canaan. Cf. Num. 13:31-14:23.
13. Lev. 19:18.
14. Reading *de'ah* with the traditional version, the Rome edition, and other editions listed in Lieberman; Hyamson has *da'at*.
15. *B.T.*, Yoma, 23a; *Sifra* to Lev. 19:18.
16. Ps. 7:5. The next verse continues: "Let the enemy pursue my soul and overtake it, and tread my life down to the earth; let him lay my glory in the dust."
17. Lev. 19:18.
18. *B.T.*, Yoma, 23a; *Sifra* to Lev. 19:18.
19. More literally: If he guards (*noter*) the thing. The primary meaning of the Hebrew word that refers to bearing a grudge is to "guard" or "keep."
20. *Masa' umatan*, a Hebrew idiom meaning literally, "carrying and giving."
21. Maimonides closes the work as he had begun, with a reference to "human beings" (*benei 'adam*) and an allusion to man's political nature. Cf. *supra*, Chapter One, note five.

II

EIGHT CHAPTERS

Eight Chapters is part of Maimonides' *Commentary on the Mishnah*. The *Mishnah* itself is an early rabbinic code of law, dating from the third century C.E. It later became part of the *Talmud*, which contains lengthy and often complicated discussions of the *Mishnah*. Maimonides' *Commentary on the Mishnah*, his first legal work, made the *Mishnah* accessible to readers who did not have extensive knowledge of the *Talmud*.

No tractate of the *Mishnah* deals with ethics as such. In order to give a coherent account of this subject, Maimonides wrote a long Introduction to *Pirqei Avot (Chapters of the Fathers)*. This Introduction, a self-contained unit with surprisingly few quotations from *Avot,* has come to be known as *Eight Chapters*. The work was not entitled *Eight Chapters* by Maimonides, but he did divide the original Arabic text into eight chapters.[1]

EIGHT CHAPTERS

INTRODUCTION

In the introduction to this composition, we explained the reason this compiler[1] placed this *tractate [Avot]* in this *Order*,[2] and we also mentioned its great utility.[3] Several times in earlier parts of this composition we promised to speak about useful matters in this *tractate* and to do so at some length. For even though it is clear and easily understood on the surface, to carry out what it contains is not easy for all people, nor are all of its intentions understandable without a lucid explanation. However, it leads to great perfection and true happiness, and I therefore saw fit to discuss it in detail.

They [the sages], peace be upon them, said: *Whoever wants to become a pious man should fulfill the words of Avot.*[4] According to us,[5] there is no rank above *piety* except for prophecy, the one leading to the other. As they said: *Piety brings about the holy spirit.*[6] Thus, from what they have said, it is clear that following the discipline[7] described in this *tractate* leads to prophecy. We shall explain the truth of this, for it encompasses[8] a large portion of morality.

Before taking up the explanation of *each particular law*, I saw fit to begin with some useful chapters, from which a man can acquire principles[9] and which will also be like a key for him to what we shall present in the commentary.

Know that the things about which we shall speak in these chapters and in what will come in the commentary are not matters invented on my own nor explanations I have originated. Indeed, they are matters gathered from the discourse[10] of the *sages*[11] in the *Midrash*,[12] the *Talmud*, and other compositions of theirs, as well as from the discourse of both the ancient and modern philosophers, and from the compositions of many men.[13] Hear the truth from whoever says it. Sometimes I have taken a complete passage from the text of a famous book. Now there is nothing wrong with that, for I do not attribute to myself what someone who preceded me said. We hereby acknowledge this and shall not indicate that "so-and-so said" and "so-and-so said," since that would be useless prolixity. Moreover, [identifying] the name of such an individual might make the passage offensive to someone without experience and make him think it has an evil inner meaning of which he is not aware. Consequently, I saw fit to omit the author's name, since my goal is to be useful to the reader. We shall explain to him the hidden meanings in this *tractate*.

I now turn to the chapters I saw fit to set forth here in accordance with my goal. There are eight chapters.

THE FIRST CHAPTER

On the soul of man and its powers

Know that the soul of man is a single soul. It has many different actions, some of which are sometimes called souls. One might therefore think, as the physicians do, that man has many souls. Even the most eminent physician stated that there are three souls: natural, vital, and psychic.[1] These are sometimes called powers and parts, so that one speaks of the parts of the soul. This terminology is frequently used by the philosophers. By saying "parts" they do not mean that the soul is divided into parts as bodies are divided into parts. Indeed, they regard the different actions of the totality of the soul as parts of a whole composed of those parts.

You know that the improvement of moral habits[2] is the same as the cure of the soul and its powers. The doctor who cures bodies needs first to know, in its entirety, the body he is curing and what the parts of the body are, I mean the body of man. And he needs to know what things make it sick so that they may be avoided and what things make it healthy so that they may be pursued. Similarly, the one who treats the soul and wishes to purify moral habits needs to know the soul in its entirety and its parts, as well as what makes it sick and what makes it healthy. Therefore I say that there are five parts of the soul: nutritive, sentient, imaginative, appetitive, and rational.

We have already indicated in this chapter that our discourse would be about the soul of man because man's nutritive part, for example, is not the same as the nutritive part belonging to a donkey or a horse. For man is nourished by the nutritive part of the human soul, a donkey is nourished by the nutritive part of the donkey's soul, and a palm tree is nourished by the nutritive part of its soul. Now, all these individuals are said to be "nourished" solely due to the equivocal character of the word, not because the meaning itself is one. Likewise, an individual man and animal are said to be "sentient" solely due to the equivocal character of the word, not because the sensation which is in man is the same sensation which is in the horse. Nor is the sensation which is in one species the same sensation which is in another species. Rather, every single species having a soul possesses a unique soul, different from the soul of another [species].

Certain actions necessarily stem from one soul and other actions from another soul. One action may resemble another action, so that the two actions are thought to be identical even though they are not. For example, consider three dark places: the sun shines upon one of them, and it is illumined; the moon rises over the second place, and it is illumined; a lamp is lit in the third place, and it is illumined. Light is found in each one of them, but the reason for the first light and its cause is the sun, the cause of the second is the moon, and the cause of the third is fire. Likewise, the cause of a man's sensation is the soul of man; the cause of a donkey's sensation is the soul of the donkey; and the cause of an eagle's sensation is the soul of the eagle. There is no notion common to all of them [the sensations] except through equivocation. Grasp this notion, for it is extraordinarily marvelous. Many pseudo-philosophers stumble over it and therefore cling to repulsive views and incorrect opinions.[3]

I return to our point about the parts of the soul. I say that the nutritive part consists in the power of attracting, retaining, digesting, excreting, growing, procreating its kind, and separating mixtures so that it isolates what should be used for nourishment and what should be excreted. The discourse concerning these seven powers, the means by which they act, how they act, in which organs their action is more obvious and evident, which [powers] are continuously in existence, and which ones cease[4] at a given time—all of this necessarily belongs to the art of medicine. There is no need to go into it in this place.

The sentient part [of the soul] consists of the five powers well known to the multitude: sight, hearing, taste, smell, and touch. The last is found in the entire surface of the body and has no specific organ like the other four powers.

The imaginative part is the power that preserves the impressions of sensibly perceived objects after they vanish from the immediacy of the senses that perceived them. Some impressions are combined with others, and some are separated from others. Therefore, from things it has perceived, this power puts together things it has not perceived at all and which are not possible for it to perceive. For example, a man imagines an iron ship floating in the air, or an individual whose head is in the heavens and whose feet are on the earth, or an animal with a thousand eyes. The imaginative power puts together many such impossible things and makes them exist in the imagination. Concerning this point the dialectical theologians[5] committed a great, repulsive error, upon which they laid the foundation of their erroneous view concerning the division of the necessary, the admissible, and the impossible. They thought, or made people fancy, that everything that can be imagined is possible.[6] They did not know that this power combines things whose existence is impossible, as we have mentioned.

The appetitive part is the power by which a man desires, or is repulsed by, a certain thing. From this power originate such actions as seeking something or fleeing from it, as well as being attracted to something or avoiding it; rage and agreeableness, fear and boldness, cruelty and compassion, love and hatred, and many such disturbances[7] of the soul. This power[8] uses all the organs of the body as instruments; for example, the power of the hand for hitting, the power of the foot for walking, the power of the eye for seeing, and the power of the heart for being bold or fearful. Likewise, the rest of the organs—both internal and external—and their powers are instruments for this appetitive power.

The rational part is the power found in man by which he perceives intelligibles,[9] deliberates, acquires the sciences, and distinguishes between base and noble actions. Some of these activities are practical and some are theoretical. Of the practical, some are productive and some are reflective. By means of the theoretical, man knows the essence[10] of the unchanging beings. These [theoretical activities] are called sciences without qualification. The productive is the power by means of which we acquire occupations, such as carpentry, agriculture, medicine, and navigation. The reflective is that by which one deliberates about a thing he wishes to do at the time he wishes to do it—whether it is possible to do it or not and, if it is possible, how it ought to be done. This is the extent to which the topic of the soul ought to be discussed here.

Know that this single soul, whose powers or parts are described above, is like matter, and the intellect is its form. If it does not attain its form, the existence of its capacity to receive this form is for nought and is, as it were, futile. This is the meaning of his [Solomon's] statement: *Indeed, without knowledge a soul is not good.*[11] He means that the existence of a soul that does not attain its form, but is rather *a soul without knowledge, is not good.* This is not the place for a discourse about form, matter, or how many intellects there are and how they are attained. It is not needed for the discourse we wish [to present] about ethics,[12] but is more appropriate for the Book of Prophecy which we have mentioned.[13] Here I terminate this chapter and begin another.

THE SECOND CHAPTER

On the disobedience[1] of the soul's powers and on knowledge of the part in which the virtues and the vices are primarily[2] found

Know that disobedience[3] and obedience[4] of the Law are found only in two parts of the soul, namely, the sentient part and the appetitive part. All the *transgressions* and the *commandments* involve these two parts. There is no obedience or disobedience in the nutritive or imaginative parts, since thought[5] and choice do not act upon them at all. By his thought[5] man is not able to suspend their action or to limit them to a certain action. Do you not see that these two parts—I mean the nutritive and the imaginative—are active during sleep unlike the other powers of the soul? Although there is perplexity concerning the rational part, I say that this power too may bring about obedience and disobedience, namely, belief in a false or a true opinion. But there is no act in it to which the terms *commandment* or *transgression* would apply. Therefore I said in what has preceded that the *transgressions* and the *commandments* are found in those two parts.

As for the virtues, there are two kinds: moral virtues and rational virtues. Opposed to them are two kinds of vices. The rational virtues are found in the rational part. Among them are: (i) wisdom, which is knowledge of the remote and proximate causes and which comes after knowledge of the existence of the thing whose causes are being investigated; and (ii) intelligence, which includes (a) the theoretical intellect, I mean, the first intelligibles,[6] which we have by nature; (b) the acquired intellect, but this is not the place for that; and (c) brilliance and excellent comprehension, that is, excellent grasp of a thing quickly, in no time, or in a very short time. The vices of this power are the contrary of these or their opposite.

The moral virtues are found only in the appetitive part, and the sentient part is in this case a servant of the appetitive part. The virtues of this part are very numerous; for example, moderation, liberality, justice, gentleness, humility, contentment, courage,[7] and others. The vices of this part consist in being deficient or excessive with regard to these [things].

Neither virtue nor vice is ascribed to the nutritive and imaginative parts. Rather, one says that they flow properly or improperly, just as one says that a given man's digestion is excellent, has stopped, or is impaired, or that his imagination is impaired or flows properly. There is neither virtue nor vice in any of these things. This is what we wished to set down in this chapter.

THE THIRD CHAPTER

On the diseases of the soul

The ancients said that the soul can be healthy or sick, just as the body can be healthy or sick.[1] The health of the soul consists in its condition and that of its parts being such that it always does good and fine things and performs noble actions. Its sickness consists in its condition and that of its parts being such that it always does bad and ugly things and performs base actions.

The health and sickness of the body are investigated by the art of medicine. Now due to the corruption of their senses, people with sick bodies imagine the sweet as bitter and the bitter as sweet. They fancy that what is suitable is not suitable; they strongly desire and take great pleasure in things that contain no pleasure at all for the healthy and which may even be painful, such as eating clay, charcoal, dirt, and things which are extremely pungent and sour, as well as similar foods which the healthy do not desire but loathe. In like manner, people with sick souls, I mean, bad and defective men, imagine bad things as good and good things as bad. The bad man always has a desire for ends that are in truth bad. Because of the sickness of his soul, he imagines them to be good.

When sick people not proficient in the art of medicine become aware of their illness, they seek out the physicians. They [the physicians] inform them of what they need to do, prohibit them from [taking] what they imagine to be pleasurable, and compel them to take vile, bitter things which will heal their bodies so that they will again delight[2] in pleasant things and loathe vile things. Similarly, those with sick souls need to seek out the wise men, who are the physicians of the soul. The latter will prohibit the bad things which they [the sick] think are good and treat them by means of the art that treats the moral habits of the soul, as we shall explain in the next chapter.

Those with sick souls who do not recognize their illness but imagine they are healthy or who recognize it but do not submit to medical treatment will meet the fate of a sick man who pursues his pleasures and does not submit to medical treatment —he will undoubtedly perish.

Those who recognize their illness and pursue their pleasures are spoken about in the true Scripture, which describes them as saying: *For in the stubbornness of my heart I walk, etc.;*[3] i.e., he intends to quench his thirst but he actually increases it.

Those who do not recognize their illness are described by *Solomon* in many places. He said: *The way of the fool is straight in his eyes, but he who listens to counsel is wise*[4]—he means the man who accepts the opinion of the wise man, who informs him of the way which is[5] truly *straight,* not the one he supposes to be *straight.* And he [Solomon] said: *There is a way which seems straight to a man, but its end is the ways of death.*[6] He said of those whose souls are sick and who do not know what is harmful or useful to them: *The way of the wicked is like darkness; they know not why they stumble.*[7]

The art of medical treatment for the soul is as I shall describe it in the fourth chapter.

THE FOURTH CHAPTER
On medical treatment
for the diseases of the soul

Good actions are those balanced in the mean between two extremes, both of which are bad; one of them is an excess and the other a deficiency. The virtues are states[1] of the soul and settled dispositions in the mean between two bad states [of the soul], one of which is excessive and the other deficient. Certain actions necessarily result from these states[1] [of the soul]. For example, moderation is the moral habit in the mean between lust and insensibility to pleasure. Thus, moderation is one of the good actions, and the state of the soul that produces moderation is a moral virtue.[2] Lust is the first extreme and total insensibility to pleasure the other extreme; both of them are completely bad. The two states of the soul necessarily giving rise to lust (the excessive state) and insensibility (the deficient state) are both moral vices. In like manner, liberality[3] is the mean between miserliness and extravagance; courage is the mean between rashness and cowardice; wit is the mean between buffoonery and dullness; humility is the mean between haughtiness and abasement; generosity[4] is the mean between prodigality and stinginess; contentment is the mean between greed and laziness; gentleness is the mean between irascibility and servility; modesty is the mean between impudence and shyness; and so too, with the rest of them. If the meanings are understood, it is not absolutely necessary that names be assigned to them.

People often err concerning these actions and think that one of the two extremes is good and a virtue of the soul. Sometimes they think the first extreme is good, as when they think rashness is a virtue and call rash men courageous. If they see an exceedingly rash and bold person in a perilous situation who intentionally throws himself into danger but is saved by chance, they praise him for it and call him courageous. Sometimes they think the other extreme is good[5] and say that someone who depreciates himself is gentle; or that a lazy man is contented; or that someone insensible to pleasure because of the dryness of his nature is moderate. Due to this kind of error, they also think that extravagance and prodigality are among the praiseworthy actions. Now all this is erroneous, for in truth one praises the mean, and a man needs to aim at it and continuously weigh all his actions with a view to this mean.

Know that these moral virtues and vices are acquired and firmly established in the soul by frequently repeating the actions pertaining to a particular moral habit over a long period of time and by our becoming accustomed to them.[6] If those actions are good, we shall acquire the virtue; if they are bad, we shall acquire the vice. Since by nature man does not possess either virtue or vice at the beginning of his life (as we shall explain in the eighth chapter), he undoubtedly is habituated from childhood to actions in accordance with his family's way of life and that of the people of his town. These actions may be in the mean, excessive, or defective—as we have indicated.

Should his soul become sick, he must follow the same course in treating it[7] as in the medical treatment for bodies. For when the body gets out of equilibrium, we look to which side it inclines in becoming unbalanced, and then oppose it with its contrary until it returns to equilibrium. When it is in equilibrium, we remove that counterbalance and revert to that which keeps the body in equilibrium. We act in a similar manner with regard to moral habits. We may, for example, see a man whose soul has reached a condition[8] in which he is miserly toward himself. This is one of the vices of the soul, and the action he performs is one of the bad actions—as we have explained in this chapter. Thus, if we wanted to give medical treatment to this sick person, we would not order him to be liberal. That would be like using a balanced course for treating someone whose fever is excessive; this would not cure him of his sickness. Indeed, this man [with a miserly soul] needs to be made to be extravagant time after time. He must repeatedly act in an extravagant manner until the condition that makes him miserly is removed from his soul, and he just about acquires an extravagant disposition or comes close to it. Then we would make him stop the extravagant actions and order him to perform liberal actions continually. He must always adhere to this course and not go toward the excess or deficiency. Similarly, if we were to see him acting in an extravagant manner, we would order him to perform miserly actions repeatedly.

But we would not make him repeat miserly actions as many times as we made him repeat extravagant actions. This subtlety is the rule of therapy and is its secret. For a man can more easily turn from extravagance to liberality than from miserliness to liberality. Likewise, it is easier to turn from being insensible to pleasure to being moderate than from being lustful to being moderate. Therefore we make the lustful man repeat actions which lack pleasure more than we make the insensible man repeat lustful actions; we require the coward to practice rashness more than we require the rash man to practice cowardice; and we train the stingy man in prodigality more than we train the prodigal man in stinginess. This is the rule for the medical treatment of moral habits, so memorize it.

Because of this teaching, the virtuous men would not let a disposition of their souls remain in the mean, but would incline a little toward the excess or the defect as a precaution. I mean, they would, for example, incline from moderation a little toward insensibility to pleasure, from courage a little toward rashness, from generosity a little toward prodigality, from humility a little toward abasement, and likewise with the rest. This is the meaning expressed in their saying, *inside the line of the law.*[9] What the virtuous men did at certain times and also what some individuals among them [always] did in inclining toward one extreme—for example, fasting, rising at night, abstaining from eating meat and drinking wine, keeping away from women, wearing garments of wool and hair, dwelling on mountains, and secluding themselves in desolate places—they did only with a view to medical treatment, as we have indicated. Again, if they saw that due to the corruption of the people of the city they would be corrupted through contact with them and through seeing their deeds and that social intercourse with them would bring about the corruption of their own moral

habits, then they withdrew to desolate places where there are
no evil men. As the prophet said, peace be upon him: *O that I
were in the desert.*[10]

When the ignorant saw these virtuous men perform such
actions, but without knowing their intention, they thought
those actions to be good and aimed at performing them,
claiming to be like those virtuous men. They set about afflicting
their bodies with every kind of affliction, thinking they were
acquiring virtue and doing something good and would thereby
come near to God—as if God were an enemy of the body and
desired its ruin and destruction. They were not aware that
those actions are bad and that one of the vices of the soul is
thereby acquired. Such men can only be compared to someone
ignorant of the art of medicine who sees that skillful physicians
have given deathly sick people the pulp of colocynth, scammony, aloe, and similar things to drink, while forbidding them
any food, and that they are cured of their disease and completely escape destruction. Such an ignorant man then says:
"Since these things cure disease, it is even more appropriate
and fitting that they preserve or augment the health of a
healthy man." He therefore proceeds to take them continuously and follows the regimen of the sick; as a result he undoubtedly becomes sick. Similarly, those with sick souls are undoubtedly
so from taking medication while they are healthy.

This perfect Law which perfects us makes no mention of
such things. As [the Psalmist] who knew it testified about it: *The
Law of the Lord is perfect, making wise the simple, restoring the
soul.*[11] Indeed, its goal is for man to be natural by following the
middle way. He shall adhere to the mean when he eats
whatever is his to eat, when he drinks whatever is his to drink,
and when he has sexual intercourse with whomever is his to
have sexual intercourse. He shall dwell in a city and follow
justice and equity; he shall not inhabit caves or mountains, nor
wear garments of hair and wool, nor torment his body or make
it weary or afflict it. That is forbidden in the tradition which has
come down to us. He [God] said about the *Nazirite*: *He [the
priest] shall make atonement for him because he sinned against the
soul.*[12] They said: *Now then, against which soul did he sin? His own,
because he withheld himself from wine. Is there not here an argument
from the lesser to the greater? If whoever afflicts himself regarding*

wine needs atonement, how much the more does the one who afflicts himself regarding everything [need atonement].[13]

In the traditions of our prophets and those who transmit our Law, we see these men aiming at the mean and at preserving their souls and bodies in accordance with what the Law requires. God (may He be exalted) answered through His prophet those who asked if they should continue fasting one day in the year or not. They said to *Zechariah: Should I weep in the fifth month, separating myself, as I have done for so many years?*[14] And He answered them: *When you fasted and mourned in the fifth and in the seventh month these seventy years, did you at all fast unto Me, even unto Me? And when you eat and you drink, are you not the ones who eat and who drink?*[15] Then He commanded them to follow only the mean and virtue, and not to fast. This is what he said to them: *Thus spoke the Lord of hosts saying: Execute true judgment and show loving-kindness and compassion, every man to his brother, etc.*[16] After that he said: *Thus says the Lord of hosts: The fast of the fourth month and the fast of the fifth and the fast of the seventh and the fast of the tenth shall be for the house of Judah joy and gladness and cheerful seasons. Love truth and peace.*[17] Know that *truth* refers to the rational virtues because they are immutably true (as we mentioned in the second chapter) and that *peace* refers to the moral virtues through which there is *peace in the world*.

I return to my purpose. If it be said by the men of our Law who imitate the [other] religious communities—and I speak only of them—that they torment their bodies and renounce their pleasures only to discipline the powers of the body so as to incline a little to one side (in the way we have explained in this chapter that a man ought to do), this is an error on their part, as we shall explain. The Law forbids what it forbids and commands what it commands only for this reason, i.e., that we move away from one side as a means of discipline. God therefore enjoined the following upon us: the prohibition of all forbidden foods, the prohibition of forbidden sexual intercourse,[18] the ban concerning the *prostitute*, the requirement of *a marriage contract* and *betrothal*, and even so [sexual intercourse] not always being permitted but forbidden during the periods of *menstruation* and *birth*, and the further limitation upon sexual intercourse instituted by our elders who prohibited it during the daytime, as we explained in *Sanhedrin*.[19] The purpose of all this is that we move very far away from the extreme of lust and go a little from the mean toward insensibility to pleasure so that the state of moderation be firmly established within our souls. The same applies to everything occurring in the Law with respect to the paying of *tithes*,[20] the *gleanings of the harvest*,[21] the *forgotten sheaves*,[22] the *corner of the field*,[23] the *fallen grapes*,[24] the *gleanings of the vineyard*,[25] the decree of the *Sabbatical year*[26] and the *Jubilee year*,[27] and *charity sufficient for what the needy lack*.[28] These come close to prodigality so that we move very far away from the extreme of stinginess and approach the extreme of prodigality, the purpose being to establish generosity firmly within us.

If you consider most of the commandments in this way, you will find that all of them discipline the powers of the soul. For example, they eliminate revenge and vengeance by His saying: *You shall not take revenge nor bear a grudge*,[29] *You shall surely release it*,[30] and *You shall surely help to lift them up, etc.*;[31] these aim at weakening the power of rage and irascibility. Similarly, *You shall surely bring them back*,[32] aims at removing the state of avarice. Similarly, the following aim at removing the state of impudence and instilling that of modesty: *You shall rise before the aged and honor the old man*,[33] *Honor your father*,[34] and *You shall not turn aside from the thing they shall tell you*.[35] Moreover, He also moves [us] away from the other extreme, i.e., shyness, for in order that shyness be eliminated and we remain in the middle way, He said: *You shall surely rebuke your neighbor and not bear sin because of him*[36] and *You shall not fear the face of any man*.[37]

Only a manifestly ignorant individual would come and wish to add to these things and, for example, prohibit eating and drinking, in addition to the stipulated prohibition about food; and prohibit marriage, in addition to what is prohibited concerning sexual intercourse; and give all of his money to the *poor* or to the *Temple property*, in addition to what the Law says about *charity*, *Temple properties*, and *valuations*.[38] His actions are bad and he does not know that he goes all the way to one extreme, completely leaving the mean. The *sages* have a statement about this subject in the *Jerusalem Talmud*, in the ninth [*tractate*] of *Nedarim*, and nothing more marvelous than it has yet reached me. They censure those who become like prisoners by imposing oaths and *vows* on themselves, and they literally say there: *Rav Aidi [said] in the name of Rabbi Isaac: Is what the Torah has prohibited for you not enough, that you prohibit other things for yourself?*[39] This is precisely the meaning we have presented, neither more nor less. Thus, it has become clear to you from everything we have discussed in this chapter that it is necessary to aim at the mean in actions and not depart from it toward one of the two extremes, except with a view to medical treatment and to opposing something with its contrary.

When the man knowledgeable in the art of medicine sees his temperament changing ever so slightly, he does not neglect the disease and let it take possession of him so that he would need an extremely strong medicine. When he knows that one of his bodily organs is weak, he takes continual care of it, avoids things harmful to it, and aims at what is useful to it so that this organ becomes healthy or so that it does not become weaker. Similarly, the perfect man needs to inspect his moral habits continually, weigh his actions, and reflect upon the state of his soul every single day. Whenever he sees his soul inclining toward one of the extremes, he should rush to cure it and not let the evil state[40] become established by the repetition of a bad action—as we have mentioned. Thus, as we said above, he should attend to the defective moral habit in himself and continually seek to cure it, for a man inevitably has defects. Indeed, the philosophers have said that it would be very difficult to find someone disposed by nature toward all of the moral and rational virtues. This has also been said frequently in the books of the prophets. He said: *Behold, He puts no trust in His servants, etc.*[41] *And how can one born of woman be just?*[42] *Solomon* said absolutely: *There is no man who is just upon the earth, who does only good and does not sin.*[43]

You know that God, may He be exalted, said to the master of the first and the last men, *Moses our master,* peace be upon him: *Because you did not believe in Me to sanctify Me,*[44] *Because you rebelled against My word,*[45] *Because you did not sanctify.*[46] His sin, peace be upon him, in all this was that he inclined toward one of the two extremes away from one of the moral virtues—i.e., gentleness—when he inclined toward irascibility and said: *Hear now you rebels.*[47] God disapproved of a man like him becoming irascible in the presence of the community of *Israel* when irascibility was not proper. For this individual something like that was a *profanation of the Name*, because they would imitate his every movement and speech and would wish thereby to attain the happiness of this world and the other [world]. How could irascibility, which (as we have explained) is among the bad actions, stem from him and not originate from one of the evil states of the soul?

We shall now explain the significance of His saying, *You rebelled against My word.*[48] He [Moses] was not addressing the vulgar nor men without virtue, but people the least significant of whose women was like *Ezekiel ben Buzi*, as the *sages* have mentioned.[49] They would reflect upon everything he would say or do. Thus when they saw him irate, they [in effect] said: "He, peace be upon him, has no moral vice, and if it were not that he knew God has become angry with us about our searching for water and that we have exasperated Him, may He be exalted, he would not have become irate."We do not find that God, may He be exalted, was irate or angry when He spoke to [Moses] about this matter. Rather, He said to him: *Take the rod . . . and you shall give the congregation and their cattle drink.*[50] We have departed from the purpose of the section, but we have solved one of the difficulties of the *Torah*. It is often spoken about and someone often asks: "What sin did he commit?" Examine what we have said and what others have said about it, and the truth will lead the way.

I return to my purpose. If a man continually weighs his actions and aims at the mean, he is in the highest of human ranks. In that way, he will come close to God and will attain what belongs to Him. This is the most perfect of the ways of worship. The *sages, may their memory be blessed*, referred to this goal, commented on it, and said: *Everyone who appraises his paths merits and sees the salvation of the Holy One, blessed be He. As it is said: "And to him who sets his way aright will I show the salvation of God."* Do not read *wesam derekh*, but *wesham derekh.*[51] *Shumah* means "assessing" and "appraising," and this is precisely the meaning that we have explained in this entire chapter. This is the extent of what we saw to be necessary with respect to this subject.

THE FIFTH CHAPTER

On directing the powers of the soul toward a single goal

Man needs to subordinate all his soul's powers to thought, in the way we set forth in the previous chapter, and to set his sight on a single goal: the perception of God (may He be glorified and magnified), I mean, knowledge of Him, in so far as that lies within man's power. He should direct all his actions, both when in motion and at rest, and all his conversation toward this goal so that none of his actions is in any way frivolous, I mean, an action not leading to this goal. For example, he should make his aim only the health of his body when he eats, drinks, sleeps, has sexual intercourse, is awake, and is in motion or at rest. The purpose of his body's health is that the soul find its instruments[1] healthy and sound in order that it can be directed toward the sciences and toward acquiring the moral and rational virtues, so that he might arrive at that goal.

On the basis of this reasoning, he would not aim at pleasure alone, choosing the most pleasant food and drink, and similarly with the rest of his conduct. Rather, he would aim at what is most useful. If it happens to be pleasant, so be it; and if it happens to be repugnant, so be it. Or he would aim at what is most pleasant in accordance with medical theory. For example, if his desire for food subsides, it should be stimulated by agreeable, pleasant, good foods. Similarly, if the humor of black bile[2] agitates him, he should make it cease by listening to songs and various kinds of melodies, by walking in gardens and fine buildings, by sitting before beautiful forms, and by things like this which delight[3] the soul and make the disturbance of black bile disappear from it. In all this he should aim at making his body healthy, the goal of his body's health being that he attain knowledge. Similarly, if he bestirs himself and sets out to acquire money, his goal in accumulating it should be to spend it in connection with the virtues and to use it to sustain his body and to prolong his existence, so that he perceives and knows of God what is possible for him to know.

On the basis of this reasoning, the art of medicine is given a very large role with respect to the virtues, the knowledge of God, and attaining true happiness. To study it diligently is among the greatest acts of worship. It is, then, not like weaving and carpentry, for it enables us to perform our actions so that they become human actions, leading to the virtues and the truths. For if a man sets out to eat appetizing food which is pleasant to the palate and which has an agreeable odor, but is harmful and could be the cause of grave illness or eventually of destruction, then this man and the beasts are alike. That is not the action of a man insofar as he is a man. Indeed, it is the action of a man insofar as he is an animal: *He is like the beasts that perish.*[4] A human action [requires] taking only what is most useful: one sometimes leaves the most pleasant aside and eats what is most repugnant, with a view to seeking what is most useful. This is an action based upon thought and distinguishes man in his actions from what is unlike him. Similarly, if he has sexual intercourse whenever he wishes, without heeding what is harmful or useful, then he performs this action insofar as he is an animal, not insofar as he is a man.

Now all of his conduct might be with a view to what is most useful, as we have mentioned, but if he makes his goal solely the health of his body and its being free from illness, he is not virtuous. For while such a man prefers the pleasure of health, another prefers the pleasure of eating or sexual intercourse, and neither has a true goal for his actions. The proper goal for all of one's conduct is the body's health and prolonging its existence in a sound manner in order that the instruments of the soul's powers—which are the organs of the body—remain sound. Then the soul can be directed toward the moral and rational virtues without any obstacle.

There is no question about [the value of] whatever he learns from the sciences and from studies insofar as they provide a way for attaining that goal. Subjects not useful for attaining that goal—such as questions of algebra, the Book of Cones, mechanics, most questions of engineering and moving weights, and many such questions—aim at sharpening the mind and training the rational power in the method of demonstration, so that a man acquires the skill of distinguishing a demonstrative syllogism from one which is not. He then possesses this method for attaining knowledge of the true reality of His existence, may He be exalted.

Similarly in all of his conversation, a man should speak only about what is useful for his soul or about what wards off harm from his soul or body, or about knowledge or[5] virtue, or to praise virtue or a virtuous man, or to censure vice or a vicious man. If the purpose of vilifying defective men and denouncing their deeds is to belittle them before the people so that they will be warned about them and not perform their actions, then that is necessary and is a virtue. Have you not seen His statement, may He be exalted: *Like the deeds of the land of Egypt where you dwelled [you shall not do] and like the deeds of the land of Canaan;*[6] and so too, the description of the Sodomites. In the *Bible,* whenever corrupt and defective individuals are censured and their deeds denounced and good men are praised and glorified, the purpose (as I mentioned to you) is for the people to follow the way of the latter and avoid the way of the former.

If a man sets this notion [i.e., knowledge of God] as his goal, he will discontinue many of his actions and greatly diminish his conversation. For someone who adheres to this goal will not be moved to decorate walls with gold or to put a gold border on his garment—unless he intends thereby to give delight to his soul[7] for the sake of its health and to drive sickness from it, so that it will be clear and pure to receive the sciences. Thus, they said: *An attractive dwelling, an attractive wife, attractive utensils, and a bed prepared for the disciples of the wise give delight to the mind of a man.*[8] For the soul becomes weary and the mind dull by continuous reflection upon difficult matters, just as the body becomes exhausted from undertaking toilsome occupations until it relaxes and rests[9] and then returns to equilibrium. In a similar manner, the soul needs to rest and to do what relaxes the senses, such as looking at beautiful decorations and objects, so that weariness be removed from it. As they said: *When our masters grew weary from study. . . .*[10] Now it is doubtful that when done for this purpose, these are bad or futile, I mean, decorating and adorning buildings, vessels, and garments.

Know that this level is very lofty and is difficult to reach. Only a few perceive it and then, only after very great discipline. So if a man happens to exist in this condition, I would not say that he is inferior to the prophets. I refer to a man who directs all the powers of his soul solely toward God, may He be exalted; who does not perform an important or trivial action nor utter a word unless that action or that word leads to virtue or to something leading to virtue; and who reflects and deliberates

upon every action and motion, sees whether it leads to that goal
or not, and then does it. This is what the Exalted requires that
we make as our purpose when He says: *And you shall love the
Lord your God with all your heart and with all your soul.*[11] He
means, set the same goal for all the parts of your soul, namely,
to love the Lord your God. The prophets, peace be upon them,
have also urged this purpose. He [Solomon] said: *In all your
ways know Him.*[12] The *sages* explained this and said: *Even with a
transgression;*[13] i.e., you should make your goal the truth when
doing such a thing, even if from a certain point of view you
commit a transgression. The *sages,* peace be upon them, summarized this whole notion in the briefest possible words and
encompassed the meaning with utmost perfection, so that if
you were to consider the brevity of those words—how they
express the greatness and magnificence of this notion in its
entirety, about which so many works have been composed
without being able to grasp it—then you would know it was
undoubtedly spoken by divine power. This is what they say in
one of their commands in this *tractate: Let all your deeds be for the
sake of Heaven.*[14] This is the notion we have explained in this
chapter and is as much as we think needs to be mentioned here
in accordance with these introductory remarks.[15]

THE SIXTH CHAPTER

On the difference between the virtuous man
and the continent man[1]

The philosophers said that even though the continent man
performs virtuous actions, he does good things while craving
and strongly desiring to perform bad actions. He struggles
against his craving and opposes by his action what his
[appetitive] power, his desire, and the state[2] of his soul arouse
him to do; he does good things while being troubled at doing
them. The virtuous man, however, follows in his action what his
desire and the state of his soul arouse him to do, and he does
good things while craving and strongly desiring them. There is
agreement among the philosophers that the virtuous man is
better[3] and more perfect than the continent man. However,[4]
they said that the continent man can take the place of the
virtuous man in most things, even though he is necessarily

lower in rank due to his desire to do something bad. Even though he does not do it, his strong desire for it is a bad state of the soul.

Solomon had said something like this. He said: *The soul of the wicked desires evil.*[5] He spoke about the joy of the virtuous in doing good things and the pain of the nonvirtuous in doing them. This is what he says: *A joy to the righteous is the doing of justice, but dismay to evil-doers.*[6] This is what appears in the speech of the Law in agreement with what the philosophers have said.

When we investigated the speech of the *sages* about this matter, we found that according to them, someone who craves and strongly desires transgressions is more virtuous and perfect than someone who does not crave them and suffers no pain in abstaining from them. They even said that the more virtuous and perfect an individual is, the stronger is both his craving for transgressions and his pain[7] in abstaining from them. They related stories in that vein. And they said: *Whoever is greater than his friend has a greater [evil] impulse than he.*[8] As if this were not enough, they said that the reward of the continent man is proportionate to his pain in restraining himself. They said: *The reward is according to the pain.*[9] Even more significant is their commanding a man to be continent and their forbidding him to say: "I would not naturally yearn to commit this transgression, even if it were not prohibited by the Law." This is what they say: *Rabban Shimon ben Gamliel says: "Let a man not say, 'I do not want to eat meat with milk, I do not want to wear mixed fabric, I do not want to have illicit sexual relations,' but [let him say] 'I want to, but what shall I do—my Father in heaven has forbidden me.'"*[10]

If the external meaning of the two accounts [i.e., by the philosophers and the Jewish sages] is understood superficially, the two views contradict one another. However, that is not the case; rather, both of them are true, and there is no conflict between them at all. For the bad things to which the philosophers referred when they said that someone who does not desire them is more virtuous than someone who does desire them and restrains himself—these are the things generally accepted[11] by all the people as bad, such as murder, theft, robbery, fraud, harming an innocent man, repaying a benefactor with evil, degrading parents, and things like these. They are the laws about which the *sages,* peace be upon them, said: *If they were not written down, they would deserve to be written down.*[12] Some of our modern wise men who suffer from the sickness of the dialectical theologians[13] call them rational laws.[14] There is no doubt that the soul which craves and strongly desires any of them is defective and that the virtuous soul neither longs for any of these bad things at all nor suffers pain from the prohibition against them.

When the *sages* said that the continent man is more virtuous and his reward is greater, they had in mind the traditional[15] laws. This is correct because if it were not for the Law, they would not be bad at all. Therefore they said that a man needs to let his soul remain attracted to them and not place any obstacle before them other than the Law. Consider their wisdom, peace be upon them, and the examples they used. For [Rabban Shimon ben Gamliel] did not say: *Let a man not say: "I do not want to kill, I do not want to steal, I do not want to lie, but I want to— but what shall I do."* On the contrary, he mentioned only traditional[15] matters: *meat with milk, mixed fabric, and illicit sexual unions.* These laws and similar ones are what God calls, *My statutes.*[16] They said: *Statutes which I have prescribed for you, you have no permission to investigate. The nations of the world argue against them and Satan criticizes them, such as the red heifer and the scapegoat, etc.*[17] Those called rational[18] by the moderns are called *commandments*[19] in the explanation of the *sages.*

Thus, from everything we have said it has become clear what the transgressions are for which, if a man has no desire, he is more virtuous than someone who desires them but restrains himself, and which [transgressions] are the opposite. This is a marvelous subtlety and a wonderful reconciliation of the two views. The texts supporting both views indicate that what we have explained is correct. The purpose of this chapter has been completed.

THE SEVENTH CHAPTER

On the veils and their meaning

In the *Midrash*[1] and the *Haggadah*[1] as well as in the *Talmud,* it is often found that some of the prophets saw God from behind many veils, while others saw Him from behind a few veils, depending upon their closeness to God and their level of prophecy. They [the sages] said that *Moses our master* saw God from behind one diaphanous veil, I mean, a transparent one. This is what they said: *He looked through a transparent glass (sefaqlaria).*[2] *Sefaqlaria* is the name of a looking glass made from a transparent body, such as beryl or glass, as we shall explain at the end of [the tractate] *Kelim.*[3] I shall now tell you what is intended by this notion.

In the second chapter we explained that some virtues are rational and some are moral. Similarly, some vices are rational, such as ignorance, stupidity, and a slow understanding; and some are moral, such as lust, arrogance, irascibility, rage, impudence, love of money, and similar things—these moral vices are very numerous. In the fourth chapter, we gave the rule for recognizing them. All these vices are veils separating man from God, may He be exalted. To explain that, the prophet said: *Only your sins have separated you from your God.*[4] He says that our sins, which (as we have mentioned) are these evil things, are veils separating us from the Exalted.

Know that no prophet prophesies until after he acquires all the rational virtues and most of the moral virtues, i.e., the most important ones. This is their saying: *Prophecy only comes to rest upon a wise, powerful, and rich man.*[5] *Wise* undoubtedly includes all of the rational virtues. *Rich* refers to one of the moral virtues, I mean, contentment, for they call the contented man *rich.* This is what they say in defining the *rich man: Who is rich? He who rejoices with his lot.*[6] That is, he is content with what time brings him, and he is not pained at what it does not bring him. Similarly, *powerful man* refers to one of the moral virtues, I mean that he governs his powers as thought dictates—as we explained in the fifth chapter. This is their saying: *Who is a powerful man? He who conquers his impulse.*[7]

To possess the moral virtues in their entirety, to the extent of not being impaired by any vice at all, is not one of the conditions of prophecy. *Solomon* was a prophet according to the testimony of Scripture: *In Gibeon the Lord appeared, etc.*[8] Yet we find that he had a moral vice, namely, manifest lust. This can be seen from the number of wives he took, which is an action stemming from the state of lust. It clearly says: *Did not Solomon sin by these things, etc.*[9] Similarly *David,* peace be upon him, was a prophet. He said: *The Rock of Israel spoke to me.*[10] Yet we find that he was cruel, even though he directed it [his cruelty] against the *Gentiles* and toward killing the infidels, while being compassionate to *Israel.* Still, it is explained in *Chronicles* that because of his frequent killing, God did not find him fit to build the *Temple* and said to him: *You shall not build a house unto My name, because you have shed much blood, etc.*[11] We find that *Elijah, may his memory be blessed,* had the moral habit of irascibility, even though he directed it against the heretics[12] and was irate at them. Still the *sages, may their memory be blessed,* explained that God removed him [from the world] and said to him: "Someone with as much zeal as you is not suitable for the people, for he would destroy them.[13] Similarly, we find that *Samuel* was afraid of *Saul,* and *Jacob* was fearful of meeting *Esau.*[14]

These moral habits and others like them are the veils of the prophets, peace be upon them. Thus, whoever has two or three moral habits not in the mean, as we explained in the fourth chapter, is said to see God from behind two or three veils. Do not fail to know that the defectiveness inherent in some moral habits diminishes the degree of prophecy. We have found that some moral vices, such as irascibility, prevent prophecy entirely. They said: *If anyone who becomes angry is a prophet, his prophecy departs from him.*[15] They infer this from *Elishah,* for when he was irascible, revelation ceased until his irascibility disappeared. This is what he said: *And now bring me a musician.*[16] The same holds for anxiety and grief, for the *holy spirit* was removed from *our father Jacob* during all the days of his sadness over *Joseph* until the news came that he was alive. It [Scripture] said: *And the spirit of Jacob their father was revived.*[17] The *Targum,* which explains the intentions transmitted by *our master Moses,* said: *The holy spirit came to rest upon Jacob their father.*[18] And there is the text of the *sages: Prophecy does not come to rest through laziness, nor through sadness, but through something joyful.*[19]

When *our master Moses* knew that no veils remained which he had not pierced and that all the moral virtues and all the rational virtues had become perfected in him, he sought to perceive the true reality of God's existence, since no obstacle remained. So he said: *Let me see Your glory.*[20] God, may He be exalted, informed him that this was not possible, due to his being an intellect existing in matter, I mean, since he was a human being. This is what He said: *For man shall not see Me and live.*[21] Between him and the perception of the true reality of God's existence there remained only one transparent veil, namely, the unseparated human intellect.[22] God favored him and granted him more perception after his request than he had had before it. God informed him that the goal was not possible for him as long as he had a body.

The true perception was referred to as *seeing a face,* for if a man sees the face of his companion, he attains an image in his soul which he will not confuse with another. However, if he sees the back [of his companion], even if he picks him out by sight, he might be in doubt and confuse him with another. Similarly, to perceive the Exalted in truth is to attain in one's soul with regard to the verity of His existence what none of the other beings share with that existence, so that one finds His existence firmly established in his soul and distinct from the existence of the other beings found in his soul. Human perception cannot reach this level of perception, but [Moses], peace be upon him, perceived a little below it. This was referred to [in the verse]: *And you shall see My back.*[23] I shall treat this subject in detail in the Book of Prophecy.[24]

When the *sages* (peace be upon them) learned that these two kinds of vices, I mean, the rational and the moral, form a veil between man and God, and that by them the degrees of the prophets may be distinguished, they said about some [disciples], on the basis of what they had observed of their knowledge and moral habits: *They are worthy of the Presence resting upon them, as upon Moses our master.*[25] Do not let the meaning of this comparison escape you, for they likened these others to [Moses] but did not regard them as equal to him, God forbid. Similarly, they spoke about others, like *Joshua,* in the way we have indicated. This is the meaning we intended to explain in this chapter.

THE EIGHTH CHAPTER

On man's inborn disposition

It is not possible for a man to possess virtue or vice by nature, from the beginning of his life, just as it is not possible for a man to possess one of the practical arts by nature. Still, it is possible to be naturally disposed toward a virtue or a vice, so that it is easier to perform the actions that accord with a [particular virtue] or a [particular vice]. For example, if his temperament is more inclined toward dryness and the substance of his brain is pure and has little moisture, memorization and understanding meanings are easier for him than for a phlegmatic individual who has much moisture in his brain. However, if the individual disposed by temperament toward this virtue is left without any instruction and none of his powers is given direction,[1] he will undoubtedly remain ignorant. Similarly, if a natural dolt with much moisture [in his brain] is instructed and made to understand, then he will attain knowledge and understand, but with difficulty and hard work. In the same manner, an individual whose heart has a temperament a little warmer than necessary will become courageous. I mean, he is disposed toward courage; and if he is trained in courage, he will easily become courageous. Another, whose heart has a temperament colder than necessary, is disposed toward cowardice and fear, so that if he is educated and habituated accordingly, he easily acquires [these traits]. If he is directed toward courage, he can, with some hard work, become courageous, but he will undoubtedly become so if he is habituated to it.

I have explained this to you so you will not think that those senseless ravings fabricated by the astrologers are true. They go so far as to claim that an individual's time of birth determines whether he possesses virtue or vice and that he is necessarily compelled to perform certain actions. You, however, should know that our Law and Greek philosophy agree that all of man's actions are given over to him—which has been verified by true proofs. There is no compulsion on him nor is there any external cause which makes him incline toward a virtue or a vice, except for his being disposed by temperament so that something is easy or difficult for him—as we have explained. There is no way at all that he is forced or hindered.

If man's actions were done under compulsion, the commandments[2] and prohibitions[2] of the Law would be nullified and they would all be absolutely in vain, since man would have no choice in what he does. Similarly, instruction and education, including instruction in all the productive arts, would necessarily be in vain and would all be futile. For according to the doctrine of those holding the above opinion,[3] there is inevitably and necessarily an external cause making man perform a certain action, learn a certain science, and acquire a certain moral habit. Reward and punishment would also be sheer injustice, not be be meted out by some of us to others nor by God to us. For if *Simon*, the killer of *Reuben*, were inevitably compelled to kill, and the latter inevitably had to be killed, why should we punish *Simon?* And how would the Exalted, *just and righteous is He*,[4] permit him to be punished for a deed which he unavoidably did and which, had he desired not to do, he would not have been able to avoid doing? All precautions, down to the very last one, would also be useless, such as those involved in building houses, procuring food, fleeing in fear, and so forth, because what had been preordained would inevitably happen. All of this is utterly absurd and false, contrary to what is grasped by the intellect and perceived by the senses, destructive of the wall around the Law, and a judgment upon God, the Exalted, as being unjust—may He be exalted above that.

The truth about which there is no doubt is that all of man's actions are given over to him. If he wishes to act he does so, and if he does not wish to act he does not; there is no compulsion whatsoever upon him. Hence it necessarily follows that commands can be given. He said: *See I have set before you this day life and good, death and evil . . . choose life.*[5]. He gave us choice about that. It necessarily follows that disobedience is punished and obedience is rewarded. *If you obey . . . and if you do not obey.*[6] It necessarily follows that there can be instruction and learning, as well as everything that involves instruction in, and habituation to, the laws. *And you shall teach them to your children, etc.*[7] *And you shall learn them and observe them in order to do them.*[8] All the precautions stipulated in the Book of Truth also necessarily follow. *And you shall make a parapet for your roof . . . if anyone fall;*[9] *Lest he die in the battle;*[10] *In what shall he sleep?*[11] *He shall not take the mill and upper millstone as a pledge.*[12] In the *Torah* and in the prophetic books there is very often something about this subject, I mean, precaution.

The statement of the *sages* saying, *Everything is in the hands of Heaven except fear of Heaven*,[13] is correct and is similar to what we have discussed. However, people often err about it and

think that a man is compelled to perform some actions which
are in fact voluntary; for instance, marrying a certain woman or
seizing a sum of money illegally. That is incorrect because if
someone takes a woman by *a marriage contract* and *betrothal* and
she is permitted to him and he marries her *to be fruitful and to
multiply*, then this is fulfilling a *commandment*; God does not
preordain performing a *commandment*. If there were some
wickedness in marrying her, it would be a *transgression*; God
does not preordain a *transgression*. The same applies to a man
who robs someone of his money, or steals it, or deceives him
about it and[14] denies it and swears an oath to him about his
money. If God had preordained that this money would go from
the possession of the latter to that of the former, He would
have preordained a *transgression*. This is not the case. Rather,
the obedience and disobedience [of the Law] can undoubtedly
be found throughout man's voluntary actions. We have already
explained in the second chapter that the commandments[15] and
prohibitions[15] of the Law concern actions which man can choose
to do or not to do. *Fear of Heaven is not in the hands of Heaven,*
but in this [appetitive] part of the soul. Indeed, it is given over
to man's choice, as we have explained. Thus, in saying *everything [is in the hands of Heaven]*, they [the sages] mean the
natural matters about which a man has no choice, such as his
being tall or short, or a rainfall or drought, or the air being
putrid or healthy—and so too with respect to everything in the
world, except for the movement and the rest of man.

When the *sages* explained that obedience and disobedience
do not take place through the power of the Exalted nor
through His volition but through the will of the individual, they
followed the text of *Jeremiah*. This is what he says: *Out of the
mouth of the Exalted proceeds neither evil (ra'ot) nor good (tov).*[16]
Ra'ot are bad things and *ṭov* good things. Thus he says God does
not preordain that man shall do either bad or good things. If
such be the case, it is proper for man to be sad and to lament
over the sins and the outrages he has committed, since he did
wrong by his own choice. He [Jeremiah] said: *Why does a living
man lament, a strong man because of his sins?*[17] Then he reconsidered and said that the medical treatment for this sickenss is in
our hands, because just as we have done wrong by our choice,
so too it is up to us to repent and to turn away from our evil

actions. So he said afterward: *Let us search and examine our ways and return to the Lord. Let us lift up our hearts with our hands to God in heaven.*[18]

The account generally accepted among the people, examples of which may be found in the discourse of the *sages* and in the texts of the books,[19] is in a way correct: man's standing up, sitting down, and all his movements derive from the volition of God, may He be exalted, and from His will. Let us suppose, for example, that someone throws a rock into the air, and it then falls down. If we say it fell down by the volition of God, this is a correct account because God wanted the whole earth to be in the center. Therefore, whenever a piece of [the earth] is thrown up, it moves toward the center; similarly, every single particle of fire moves upward through the volition that occurred in the past making fire move upward. It is not the case that now, when this piece of the earth is in motion, God wishes it to move down.

The dialectical theologians disagree with this. I have heard them say that volition with respect to each thing takes place one moment after another, continuously.[20] We do not believe that; rather, volition occurred during *the six days of Creation,*[21] and [since then] all things act continuously in accordance with their natures. As [Solomon] said: *What was is what will be; what has been done is what will be done; there is nothing new under the sun.*[22] Therefore the *sages* insisted that there was a prior volition, during *the six days of Creation,*[23] for all the miracles which deviate from custom and which have come about or will come about as has been promised. At that time the natures of those things were determined in such a way that what has taken place in them would take place. When it takes place at the time it is supposed to, something new is presumed to occur, but that is not so. They expounded at length upon this subject in *Midrash Qohelet* and in other places. One of their sayings concerning this subject is: *The world goes along according to its custom.*[24] In all that they say, peace be upon them, you will always find they avoid positing volition in each particular thing and at each particular moment. Thus it is said of man that when he stands up and sits down, he stands up and sits down by the volition of God. This means that at the beginning of man's existence, He determined his nature in such a way that he would stand up and sit down by his own choice, not that He now wishes when he stands up that

he stand up or that he not stand up. So too, He does not wish
now, when this stone is falling down, that it fall down or not fall
down.

To sum up the matter, you should believe that just as God
wishes man to be erect in stature, broad-chested, and to have
fingers, so too He wishes him to move or be at rest of his own
accord and to perform actions voluntarily. He does not force
him to perform them nor prevent him from performing them.
This notion was explained in the Book of Truth, where He
said: *Behold, the man has become like one of us, knowing good and
evil.*[25] The *Targum* has already made clear the interpretation of
His appraisal, [*like one*] *of us, knowing good and evil.* It means that
he [Adam] has become unique in the world, i.e., a species
having no similar species with which he shares this quality he
has attained. What is this quality? It is that he himself, of his
own accord, knows the good and the bad things, does whatever
he wishes, and is not prevented from doing them. Since this is
so, he might stretch out his hand, take from this tree,[26] *and eat
and live forever.*[27] Since this is necessary for human existence, I
mean, that man performs good and bad actions by his choice
when he wishes, it necessarily follows that he can be instructed
in the good ways and be commanded, forbidden, punished,
and rewarded. All of this is just. It is necessary for him to
accustom his soul to good actions until he acquires the virtues,
and to avoid bad actions until the vices disappear from him, if
he has acquired any. He should not say he has already attained
a condition that cannot possibly change, since every condition
can change from good to bad and from bad to good; the choice
is his. With a view to this subject and for its sake, we set down
everything we discussed concerning obedience and disobedience.

Something still remains for us to explain regarding this
subject. There are some verses which lead people to fancy that
God preordains and compels disobedience. That is false and we
shall explain these verses because people are often preoccupied
with them. One of them is His saying to *Abraham: And they shall
be enslaved and oppressed.*[28] They said: "He preordained that the
Egyptians would oppress the *seed of Abraham*. Why then did He
punish them, when they necessarily and inevitably enslaved
them [the Hebrews] as He preordained?" The answer is that

this is like the Exalted saying that some people born in the future will be sinful, some will be obedient, some virtuous, and some bad. Now, this is correct, but it does not necessarily follow from this statement that a given bad man is bad without fail, nor that a given virtuous man is virtuous without fail. Rather, whoever is bad is so by his own choice. If he wishes to be virtuous, he can be so; there is nothing preventing him. Similarly, if any virtuous man wishes to, he can be bad; there is nothing preventing him. The prediction is not about a particular individual, so that he could say: "It has been preordained for me." Rather, it is stated in a general way, and each individual remains able to exercise his choice upon his original inborn disposition. Similarly, if any individual Egyptian who oppressed them and treated them unjustly had not wanted to oppress them, he had choice about that; for it was not preordained that a given individual would oppress them.

This answer is the same as the answer to the problem posed by His saying: *Behold, you are about to sleep with your fathers, and this people will rise up and go astray after the foreign gods of the land.*[29] There is no difference between this and His saying: thus we shall act toward and deal with whoever *worships idols.* If there were never anyone who committed a transgression, then the threats, all of the *curses,* and likewise all of the punishments which are in the Law would be futile. The existence of the judgment of *death by stoning* in the *Torah* does not make us say that the man who profaned the Sabbath is compelled to profane it, nor do the *curses* force us to say that those *idol worshippers,* upon whom these *curses* fell, were preordained to idol worship. Rather, everyone who worshipped [idols] did so by choice and punishment befell him. *Just as they have chosen their ways . . . I too shall choose, etc.*[30]

His saying, *And I will harden Pharaoh's heart*[31]—and then punishing him and destroying him—contains a subject for discussion and a major principle[32] stems from it. Reflect upon my discourse on this subject, set your mind to it, compare it with the discourse of everyone who has discussed it, and choose the best for yourself. If *Pharaoh* and his followers had committed no other sin than not letting *Israel* go free, the matter would undoubtedly be problematic, for He had prevented them from setting [Israel] free. As He said: *For I have hardened his heart and the heart of his servants.*[33] Then [according to this assumption] He requested that [Pharaoh] set them free, though he was compelled not to set them free. Then He punished him and destroyed him and his followers for not setting them free. This would have been an injustice and contrary to everything we have previously set forth.

However,[34] the matter is not like this, but rather *Pharaoh* and his followers disobeyed by choice, without force or compulsion. They oppressed the foreigners who were in their midst and treated them with sheer injustice. As it is clearly said: *And he said to his people: Behold, the people of Israel. . . . Come, let us deal shrewdly with them.*[35] This action was due to their choice and to the evil character of their thought; there was nothing compelling them to do it. God punished them for it by preventing them from repenting so that the punishment which His justice required would befall them. What prevented them from repentance was that they would not set [Israel] free. God explained this to [Pharaoh] and informed him that if He had only wanted to take [Israel] out [of Egypt], He would have exterminated [Pharaoh] and his followers, and they would have gone out. But in addition to taking them out, He wanted to punish [Pharaoh] for oppressing them previously. As He had said at the very outset: *And also that nation, whom they shall serve, will I judge.*[36] It was not possible to punish them if they repented, so they were prevented from repenting and they continued holding [Israel]. This is what He says: *Surely now I have put forth my hand . . . but because of this I have left you standing, etc.*[37]

No disgrace need be attached to us because of our saying that God may punish an individual for not repenting, even though He leaves him no choice about repentance. For He, may He be exalted, knows the sins, and His wisdom and justice impose the extent of the punishment. He may punish in this world alone, He may punish in the other [world] alone, or He may punish in both realms. His punishment in this world varies: He may punish with regard to the body, money, or both. He may impede some of man's voluntary movements as a means of punishment, like preventing his hand from grasping, as He did with *Jeroboam*,[38] or the eye from seeing, as He did with the *men of Sodom* who had united against *Lot*.[39] Similarly, He may prevent the choice of repentance so that a man does not at all incline toward it and is destroyed for his sin. It is not necessary for us to know His wisdom to the extent of knowing why He punished this individual with this kind of punishment and did not punish him with another kind, just as we do not know the reason he determined this species to have this form and not another form. But the general rule is *that all of His ways are just.*[40] He punishes the sinner to the extent of his sin and He rewards the beneficent man to the extent of his beneficence.

If you were to say: "Why did He request, time after time, that [Pharaoh] set *Israel* free, although he was prevented from doing so? It is as though the plagues came down upon him for remaining obstinate, although his punishment—as we have said —was that he remain obstinate. Was it not futile, then, to request of him what he was unable to do?" However, this too was part of God's wisdom, to teach [Pharaoh] that if God wanted to abolish his choice He would do so. So He [as it were] said to him: "I request that you set them free, and if you set them free now,[41] you will be saved. But you will not set them free so that you will be destroyed." [Pharaoh] would have had to respond favorably, which would have been the opposite of the prophet's claim that he was prevented from responding favorably. Thus, he was not able to. There is an important verse about that, well known to all the people. He said: *And for the sake of declaring My name throughout all the earth.*[42] God may punish a man by preventing him from choosing a certain action, and he knows it but is unable to struggle with his soul and drive it back to make this choice.

The punishment of *Sihon King of Heshbon* took place in the same manner, for God punished him for his previous transgression—to which he was not compelled—by preventing him from yielding to *Israel,* and so they killed him. This is what He said: *But Sihon King of Heshbon did not let us pass by him; for the Lord your God hardened his spirit, etc.*[43] Now what made this so difficult for all the commentators was their supposition[44] that *Sihon* was punished for not letting *Israel* pass through his country. They said: "Why was he punished, if he was under compulsion?"—just as they supposed that *Pharaoh* and his followers were punished because he did not set *Israel* free. The matter is precisely as we have explained. *Pharaoh* and his

followers, due to their previous oppression [of Israel], had as
their punishment from God that they not repent in order that
all those plagues would come down upon them. *Siḥon*, due to
that previous oppression or injustice in his kingdom, was
punished by being prevented from yielding to *Israel*, and so
they killed him.[45]

God already explained through *Isaiah* that He, may He be
exalted, might punish some sinners by preventing them from
repenting and not leaving them any choice about it. As He said:
*Make the heart of this people fat, and make their ears heavy [and shut
their eyes; lest they, seeing with their eyes and hearing with their ears
and understanding with their heart,] return and be healed.*[46] This is a
clear text not needing interpretation; indeed, it is a key to many
locks.

The following statement of *Elijah*, peace be upon him,
against the heretics of his age is in accordance with this
principle:[47] *For you have turned their heart backward.*[48] He means
that because they were disobedient by their will, Your punishment for them was to remove their hearts from the path of
repentance and not to leave them choice or will to abandon this
disobedience. Because of that, they continued in their heresy.
He said: *Ephraim is joined to idols; let him alone.*[49] That is, he is a
friend of the idols by his choice and he loves them. His
punishment is to be left loving them, which is the meaning of *let
him alone.* This belongs to the finest commentaries, for whoever
understands the subtlety of meanings.

Isaiah's statement, *O Lord, why do You make us stray from Your
ways and harden our heart against fear of You,*[50] is dissociated from
this whole subject and is not connected with anything involving
this notion. The intention of that statement, as can been seen
from its context, was to complain about the *Exile*, our being
strangers, our being cut off, and the victory of the [other]
religious communities over us. So he said in a pleading manner: "O Lord, when they see this victory by the heretics, they
will stray from the way of the truth, and their hearts will turn
away from fear of You. It is as if You were the one who causes
these ignorant ones to move away from the truth." That is
similar to the statement of *Moses our master: Then the nations that
have heard of Your fame will say . . . "Because the Lord was not*

able. . . ."[51] Accordingly, he [Isaiah] said afterward: *Return, for Your servants' sake, the tribes of Your inheritance*;[52] he means, so that no *profanation of the Name* occur there.

In the *minor prophets*, there is an explanation of what was said by the followers of the truth conquered by the *Gentiles* during the time of the *Exile*. Reporting what they said, he [Malachi] said: *Everyone that does evil is good in the sight of the Lord, and He delights in them; or where is the God of justice?*[53] He also reported what we have said about the severity of the *Exile*: *You have said: "It is vain to serve God; what benefit is there in keeping His charge and in walking mournfully because of the Lord of hosts? And now we deem the proud blessed, etc.*"[54] So he explained and said that He, may He be exalted, will explain the truth. And he said: *Then shall you again discern [between the righteous and the wicked]*.[55]

We have surely explained the meaning of those difficult *verses* in the *Torah* and the *Bible* which make [people] fancy that God compels disobedience. It is an explanation that is correct according to the most rigorous reflection, and we preserve our principle[56] that obedience and disobedience are in man's hands and that he is a free agent in his actions. What he wants to do, he does; what he does not want to do, he does not do. However, God punishes him for his sin by nullifying his volition, as we have explained.[57] Acquisition of the virtues and the vices is [also] in his hands. Therefore it is obligatory and necessary that he be avid and work hard for his own sake to acquire the virtues, since there is no one outside of himself moving him toward them. This is what they say in the moral teachings of this *tractate: If I am not for myself, who will be for me?*[58]

With respect to this subject, only one notion must still be briefly spoken about for the purpose of the chapter to be completed. Although I did not want to speak about it at all, necessity forces me to consider God's knowledge of the things that come into being. For that is the argument made against us by the one who claims that man is compelled to obedience and disobedience and that in all of man's actions he has no choice, since his choice depends upon God's choice. What prompts this belief is that he [the adversary] says: "Did God know whether this individual would be decent or depraved, or did He not know?" If you were to say "He knew," it would follow that he was compelled to this condition which God knew previously, or else His knowledge would not be true knowledge. If you were to say, "He did not know that previously," extremely repulsive things would follow and walls would be torn down.

Listen to what I shall say and ponder it well; without a doubt it is the truth. In divine science, I mean, metaphysics, it has already been explained that God, may He be exalted, does not know by means of knowledge nor is He alive by means of life, such that He and the knowledge are two things, like man and his knowledge. Indeed, man is different from knowledge and knowledge different from man, and they are thus two [different] things. If God were to know by means of knowledge, there would necessarily be multiplicity and the eternal things would be multiple—God, the knowledge by which He knows, the life by which He is alive, the power by which He is powerful, and likewise with all of His attributes. I have mentioned only a simple proof to you, one which comes close to the understanding of the common people. However,[59] the arguments and proofs which nullify this [i.e., the adversary's position] are very strong and are demonstrative. It is correct that He (may He be exalted) is identical with His attributes and His attributes are identical with Him, so that one says that He is the Knowledge, the Knower, and the Known; He is Life, the Living, and the one who prolongs His living essence; and likewise with the rest of the attributes. These are difficult notions. Do not desire to understand them perfectly from two or three lines of my discourse. Indeed, only a report about them is given to you.

Due to this major principle,[60] it is not permitted to say in Hebrew, *Hei Adonai* [the life of the Lord], as they say *Hei Nafshekha*[61] [the life of your soul] or *Hei Far'oh*[62] [the life of Pharaoh], i.e., the genitive construction. For the noun in the genitive case and the noun to which it is related are two different things, and a thing cannot be put into a genitive construction with itself. Because the life of God is His essence and His essence is His life and nothing other than He, they did not speak of it by means of a genitive construction. Rather, they said: *Hai Adonai*[63] [the Lord lives]. The intention is that He and His life[64] are one thing.

It has also become clear in metaphysics that by our intellects we are unable to attain perfect comprehension of His existence, may He be exalted. This is due to the perfection of His existence and the deficiency of our intellects. His existence has no causes by which He could be known. The inadequacy of our intellects to perceive Him is like the inadequacy of the light of [our] vision to perceive the light of the sun. That is not due to the weakness of the light of the sun, but to the latter being stronger than the light [of vision] which wants to perceive it. This subject has been frequently discussed, and all the discourses are correct and clear.

It therefore follows that we do not know His knowledge either, nor do we comprehend it in any way, since He is His knowledge and His knowledge is He. This idea is strange and marvelous, but it eluded them so they perished.[65] Although they knew that His existence (may He be exalted) could not be perceived in all its perfection, they sought to perceive His knowledge so that it would fall within their intellects. This is impossible, since if we were to comprehend His knowledge, we would comprehend His existence—because the whole is one thing. To perceive Him perfectly would be to perceive [Him] as He is in His existence with respect to knowledge, power, volition, life, and His other noble attributes. Thus we have explained that speculation about perceiving His knowledge is sheer ignorance. However, we know that He knows, just as we know that He exists. So if we are asked how He is identical with His knowledge, we shall say that we do not perceive that, just as we do not perceive His existence perfectly. He who wished to perceive His knowledge (may He be exalted) was rebuked and he was told: *Can you find out the deep things of God?*[66]

It follows from everything we have said that the actions of man are entrusted to him and that it is up to him to be virtuous or wicked, without God compelling him to either of these conditions. It therefore follows that there can be commands, instruction, precaution, reward, and punishment. There is no uncertainty concerning all that. As we have explained, our intellects are unable to represent His knowledge, may He be exalted, or His perception of all things.

This is the totality of what we intended to summarize in this section. It now behooves me to terminate the discourse and to begin the commentary on the *tractate* to which we prefaced these chapters.

NOTES

PREFACE

1. In the Commentary on *Avot*, Maimonides simply calls this work, "the preceding chapters." Elsewhere he refers to it as "Chapters on *Avot*" (*Commentary on the Mishnah*, Kelim, XXX 2) and "Commentary on *Avot*" (*C.M.*, Menaḥot, IX 6), as well as "Introduction to *Avot*" (*Guide*, III 35 [76b25]). The *Commentary on the Mishnah* is cited in the notes as *C.M.*

INTRODUCTION

1. R. Judah the Prince, the rabbinic sage who compiled the *Mishnah*.
2. *Neziqin*, one of the six Orders of the *Mishnah*.
3. *C.M.*, Introduction (Kafih, pp. 29–31). Maimonides says there that *Avot* sets down the chain of tradition through which the Law has been transmitted and authenticated. (Concerning the importance of the chain of tradition for establishing the authority of the Law, see *infra, Logic*, VIII, p. 156.) He also says that *Avot* describes the moral conduct of the sages, who serve as models for the rest of the people.
4. *Babylonian Talmud* (cited henceforth as *B.T.*), Baba Qamma, 30a.
5. Reading *'indanā* with the Arabic Introduction in Gorfinkle and with Ibn Tibbon (*'etzleinu*), instead of *'indā* (Kafih). The readings from Ibn Tibbon are taken from the critical edition published by J. Gorfinkle (New York: Columbia University Press, 1912).
6. *B.T.*, 'Avodah Zarah, 20b. The passage there reads: "Piety brings about humility; humility brings about fear of sin; fear of sin brings about holiness; holiness brings about the holy spirit."
7. *Ādāb*, which can also refer to good manners. In *C.M.*, Avot, IV 10, he contrasts *al-ādāb* with what is obligatory.
8. Reading *mushtamalah* (Gorfinkle), instead of *mushtalamah* (Kafih).
9. Or: premises (*muqaddimāt*).
10. Literally: speech. The word *kalām*, meaning literally "speech," is sometimes rendered as "discourse."
11. *Hakhamim*, translated as "wise men" in *M.T.*, Laws Concerning Character Traits.
12. The text has the plural: *Midrashot*.
13. For the importance of al-Fārābī's *Fuṣūl al-Madanī* ("Aphorisms of the Statesman") as one of the "modern" (Muslim) philosophic sources used by Maimonides, see Herbert Davidson, "Maimonides' *Shemonah Peraqim* and Alfarabi's *Fuṣūl al-Madanī*," *Pro-*

ceedings of the American Academy for Jewish Research XXXI (1963), pp. 33–50.

THE FIRST CHAPTER

1. The reference is probably to Galen. See Herbert Davidson, *op. cit.*, p. 37, n. 10. Maimonides accepts this tripartite division of the soul as having a certain validity. See, e.g., *Guide*, III 12 (21b). In one of his medical works, he says that the natural power is strengthened by nourishment, the vital power by music and cheerful news, and the psychic power by pleasant odors. These three powers have a bodily basis in spirits of fine vapor. The natural spirit is the vapor in the liver's blood; the vital spirit is the vapor in the heart's blood; the psychic spirit is found in the vapors of the brain. *Fī Tadbīr As-Sihhat (On the Management of Health)*, ed. H. Kroner, pp. 32, 42–43; English trans. by A. Bar-Sela, H. Hoff, and E. Faris in *Transactions of the American Philosophical Society*, LIV, 4 (July 1964), pp. 22, 27.
2. *Improvement of Moral Habits (Islāh al-Akhlāq)* is the title of a book by Solomon ibn Gabirol, an eleventh century Spanish Jewish thinker.
3. Reading *ārā'* (Wolff), instead of *ārī* (Kafih).
4. Reading *yanqadi* with Wolff and Ibn Tibbon (*yikhleh*), instead of *yaqtadī* (Kafih).
5. *Mutakallimūn* or proponents of the *Kalām*. They tried to defend the Islamic faith against rationalist attacks and often became entangled in pseudo-philosophic arguments.
6. Cf. the tenth premise in *Guide*, I 73.
7. Or: accidents (*'awārid*).
8. Reading *al-qūwah* (Wolff), instead of *al-qūwā* (Kafih).
9. Literally: he intellects.
10. Literally: according to what they are.
11. Prov. 19:2.
12. Literally: moral habits.
13. *C.M.*, Sanhedrin, X 2 (Kafih, p. 213). Maimonides later abandoned his plan to write this work and replaced it with the *Guide*. See *Guide*, Introduction (5b–6a).

THE SECOND CHAPTER

1. The text has the plural.
2. Reading *awwalan* (Wolff), instead of *aw lah* (Kafih). Although this reading is preferable, a question remains as to why Maimonides refers here to one part of the soul, but in the chapter itself, to two parts of the soul containing the virtues and vices.

3. The text has the plural.
4. The text has the plural.
5. Or: opinion (*ra'y*).
6. See *infra, Logic,* VIII, p. 156.
7. There probably was an additional virtue at this point in the original text, but it cannot be identified with certainty. Kafih has the impossible reading, *al-jubn,* "cowardice" (or *al-ghabn,* "fraud"). A number of manuscripts read *al-jidd,* "seriousness" or "eagerness." (E.g., Bibliothèque Nationale, Manuscrit Hébreu 579 and Epstein 4/57; British Museum, Oriental 2393; Oxford, Bodleian, 404, 1.) Ibn Tibbon renders the virtue in question as *'emunah,* which usually means "faithfulness" or "faith" and can connote "firmness" and "strength" (e.g., Exod. 17:12). Wolff does not have an additional virtue at this point in the text.

THE THIRD CHAPTER

1. "It is a well-known saying of the philosophers that the soul can be healthy or sick, just as the body can be healthy or sick." *Fuṣūl Mūsā fī al-Ṭibb* (*The Chapters of Moses on Medicine*), Section XXV, Ch. 40, beg. Arabic text and English trans. by J. Schacht and M. Meyerhof in *Bulletin of the Faculty of the Arts,* Cairo, V 1 (May 1937), pp. 65 and 78.
2. Reading *li-istityāb* (Wolff), instead of *li-istīṭab* (Kafih).
3. Deut. 29:18.
4. Prov. 12:15.
5. Omitting *yaẓunnuh* with Wolff and Ibn Tibbon.
6. Prov. 14:12.
7. Prov. 4:19.

THE FOURTH CHAPTER

1. Reading *hai'āt* with Wolff and Ibn Tibbon (*tekhunot*), instead of *hai'ah* (Kafih).
2. Reading *faḍīlah* with Wolff and Ibn Tibbon (*ma'alat*), instead of *faḍā'il* (Kafih).
3. Liberality (*sakhā'*) refers to the right attitude in spending money on oneself. Thus, at the deficient extreme, a man is "miserly toward himself" (*Eight Chapters,* IV, *supra,* p. 68, Kafih, p.381). Cf. *M.T.,* Laws Concerning Character Traits, I 1, where the two extremes concerning the expenditure of money upon oneself are described.
4. Generosity (*karam*) is the right disposition in giving good things to other people. The following are among the commandments which help instill generosity (*karam*): the remission of debts on the Sabbatical and Jubilee years; leaving the gleanings and a

corner of the field for the poor. (See *Eight Chapters, IV, supra,* p. 72, Kafih, p. 385). Regarding the difference between generosity (*karam*) toward other people and liberality (*sakhā'*) toward oneself, cf. Abraham Maimonides, *The High Ways to Perfection,* ed. and trans. by S. Rosenblatt (New York: Columbia University Press, 1927), Vol. I, pp. 170–71.

5. Reading *khair* with Wolff and Ibn Tibbon (*tov*); missing in Kafih.
6. Reading *lahā* (Wolff), instead of *lahumā* (Kafih).
7. Reading *fī tibbih* with Wolff and Ibn Tibbon (*birefu'ato*); missing in Kafih.
8. Reading as *hai'ah* with Wolff.
9. Cf. *M.T.,* Laws Concerning Character Traits, I 5, where those identified here as "virtuous men" (*fudalā'*) are called "pious men" (*hasidim*). Ibn Tibbon translates *fudalā'* throughout as *hasidim*.
10. Jer. 9:1.
11. Ps. 19:8. The original verse reads: "The Law of the Lord is perfect, restoring the soul; the testimony of the Lord is sure, making wise the simple."
12. Num. 6:11.
13. *B.T.,* Ta'anit 11a; Nedarim, 10a; Nazir, 19a, 22a; Baba Qamma, 91b.
14. Zech. 7:3.
15. Zech. 7:5–6.
16. Zech. 7:9.
17. Zech. 8:19.
18. The text has the plural.
19. *C.M.,* Sanhedrin, VII 4 (Kafih, pp. 181–82).
20. Deut. 14:22–29; 26:12–13.
21. Lev. 19:9; 23:22.
22. Deut. 24:19.
23. Lev. 19:9; 23:22.
24. Lev. 19:10.
25. *Ibid.*
26. Deut. 15:1–2.
27. Lev. 25:8–55.
28. This refers not simply to giving charity to the poor, but to giving a man what he "lacks," which partially depends upon his previous circumstances. Thus, if a rich man is impoverished, what he "lacks" must be restored to him—even a horse to ride upon and a servant to run before it. *M.T.,* Laws of Gifts for the Poor, VII 3.
29. Lev. 19:18.
30. Exod. 23:5. The complete verse reads: "If you see the ass of your enemy lying under its burden, you shall refrain from leaving him with it; you shall surely release it with him."
31. Deut. 22:4. The complete verse reads: "You shall not see your brother's ass or his ox fallen down by the way, and hide yourself from them; you shall surely help him to lift them up."

32. Deut. 22:1. The complete verse reads: "You shall not see your brother's ox or his sheep driven away, and hide yourself from them; you shall surely bring them back to your brother."
33. Lev. 19:32.
34. Exod. 20:12.
35. Deut. 17:11.
36. Lev. 19:17.
37. Deut. 1:17.
38. *Temple property* is property dedicated to the Temple; *valuation* refers to the monetary value of an individual's life which he may vow to dedicate to the Temple. The latter sum is fixed by the individual's age and could never exceed 50 shekels. A man is forbidden to dedicate more than one-fifth of his property to the Temple or to give more than one-fifth of his wealth to the poor. *M.T.*, Laws of Valuations and Dedicated Objects, I 3 and VIII 12.
39. *Jerusalem Talmud*, Nedarim, IX 1.
40. Reading *al-hai'ah* (Wolff), instead of *al-hai'āt* (Kafih).
41. Job 4:18. The speaker is Eliphaz.
42. Job 25:4. The original verse reads: "How can man be just with God; and how can one born of woman be clean?" The speaker is Bildad.
43. Eccles. 7:20. Maimonides reverses the word order of the first two words in the verse and thus renders it more smoothly.
44. Num. 20:12.
45. Num. 20:24.
46. Deut. 32:51.
47. Num. 20:10.
48. Num. 20:24.
49. *Mekhilta* on Exod. 15:2; *Deuteronomy Rabbah* VII 9. The prophet Ezekiel is referred to.
50. Num. 20:8.
51. *B.T.*, Mo'ed Qatan, 5a. The biblical verse is from Ps. 50:23 and, according to this interpretation of the sages, would read: "And to him who appraises his way (*wesham derekh*) will I show the salvation of God."

THE FIFTH CHAPTER

1. Reading *ālātahā* (Wolff), instead of *ālatahā* (Kafih).
2. Melancholia.
3. Or: broaden.
4. Ps. 49:13 and 49:21.
5. Adding *aw* with Wolff and Ibn Tibbon (*ow*); missing in Kafih.
6. Lev. 18:3.
7. Or: broaden his soul.

8. *B.T.*, Berakhot, 57b; Shabbat, 25b. The last part of this quotation is more literally, "broaden the mind of a man."
9. Reading *yaskun* with Wolff and Ibn Tibbon (*yinafesh*), instead of *yakun* (Kafih).
10. Source unknown.
11. Deut. 6:5.
12. Prov. 3:6.
13. *B.T.*, Berakhot, 63a.
14. *Mishnah*, Avot, II 15.
15. Or: principles (*muqaddimāt*).

THE SIXTH CHAPTER

1. Literally: the one who restrains his soul (or his desire). For Aristotle's discussion of continence, see *Nicomachean Ethics*, Book VII.
2. Reading as *hai'ah* with Wolff.
3. Literally: more virtuous.
4. Reading *lākinnahum* (Wolff), instead of *lākinnah* (Kafih).
5. Prov. 21:10.
6. Prov. 21:15.
7. Reading *kān shawquh li al-maʿāsīy wa taʿallumuh* (Wolff), and omitting *min alladhī lā yahūʿuhā wa lā yataʿallam* (Kafih). Kafih translates in accordance with the reading in Wolff, so the error is apparently due to the typesetter; a clause that occurs two lines earlier is repeated.
8. *B.T.*, Sukkah, 52a.
9. *Mishnah*, Avot, V 19.
10. Cf. *Sifra* to Lev. 20:26, where a similar statement is attributed to R. Elazer ben Azariah. "Mixed fabric" (*shaʿtnez*) contains a mixture of linen and wool.
11. Or: well-known (*al-mashhūrah*). Concerning "generally accepted opinions" (*al-mashhūrāt*), see *infra*, *Guide*, I 2, II 33; *Logic*, VIII.
12. *B.T.*, Yoma, 67b. The original passage reads: "If the following were not written down, it would be appropriate for them to be written down: [laws concerning] idolatry, illicit sexual unions, murder, robbery, the blessing of the Name." The last is a rabbinic euphemism for blasphemy. These are five of the seven commandments enjoined upon Noah and his descendants. The other two are the establishment of law courts and the prohibition against eating a limb cut off from a living animal. For Maimonides' discussion of the seven Noahidic commandments, see *M.T.*, Laws of Kings and Their Wars, IX.
13. *Mutakallimūn*. See *Eight Chapters*, I, note five.
14. More literally: intellectual laws (*al-sharāʿiʿ al-ʿaqliyah*). The noun is

the plural of the word Maimonides uses to designate the divine Law, the Torah (*al-sharī'ah*). The adjective has the same root as such words as "intellect" (*'aql*) and "intelligible" (*ma'qūl*). Saadia, the tenth-century Jewish sage, thought that there are such laws (*The Book of Doctrines and Beliefs*, III 2).

15. *al-sam'īyah.* This word has a connotation similar to the word *al-maqbūlāt*, translated as "traditions" in *Logic*, VIII.
16. Cf. *infra, Guide,* III 26.
17. *B.T.,* Yoma, 67b. Concerning the use of the red heifer for the purification from sin, see Num. 19:2–10, and for the use of the scapegoat as an atonement for sin, see Lev. 16:5–10.
18. Cf. note fourteen.
19. *Mitzvot.*

THE SEVENTH CHAPTER

1. The text has the plural: *Midrashot* and *Haggadot.*
2. *B.T.,* Yevamot, 49b.
3. *C.M.,* Kelim, XXX 2. This tractate is in a later part of the *Mishnah.*
4. Isa. 59:2.
5. *B.T.,* Shabbat, 92a. The original passage reads: "The *Shekhinah* only comes to rest upon a wise, powerful, and rich man." Cf. *B.T.,* Nedarim, 38a.
6. *Mishnah,* Avot, IV 1.
7. *Ibid.*
8. I Kings 3:5.
9. Neh. 13:26.
10. II Sam. 23:3.
11. I Chron. 22:8.
12. Or: the infidels (*al-kuffār*).
13. Cf. *B.T.,* Sanhedrin, 113.
14. I Sam. 16:2; Gen. 32:8.
15. *B.T.,* Pesaḥim, 66b.
16. II Kings 3:15.
17. Gen. 45:27.
18. The *Targum* is the Aramaic translation of the *Pentateuch.*
19. *B.T.,* Pesaḥim, 117a. The original passage reads: "The *Shekhinah* does not come to rest through laziness, nor through sadness, nor through laughter, nor through levity, nor through idle words, but through something joyful [involving] a commandment." Cf. *B.T.,* Shabbat, 31a.
20. Exod. 33:18.
21. Exod. 33:20.
22. I.e., not separated from the body.
23. Exod. 33:23.

24. See *Eight Chapters*, I, note thirteen.
25. *B.T.*, Sukkah, 28a; Baba Batra, 134a.

THE EIGHTH CHAPTER

1. Reading *tahaddā* (Wolff), instead of *tuthār* (Kafih).
2. The text has the singular.
3. I.e., that of the astrologers.
4. Deut. 32:4.
5. Deut. 30:15, 19.
6. Cf. Deut. 11:27–28.
7. Deut. 11:19.
8. Deut. 5:1.
9. Deut. 22:8. The complete verse reads: "When you build a new house, you shall make a parapet for your roof, that you do not bring the blood-guilt upon your house, if anyone fall from it."
10. Deut. 20:5–7. These verses read: "Then the officers shall speak to the people, saying, 'What man is there who has built a new house and has not dedicated it? Let him go back to his house, lest he die in the battle and another man dedicate it. And what man is there who has planted a vineyard and has not enjoyed its fruit? Let him go back to his house, lest he die in the battle and another man enjoy its fruit. And what man is there who has betrothed a wife and has not taken her? Let him go back to his house, lest he die in the battle and another man take her.' "
11. Exod. 22:26. The complete passage reads: "If you take your neighbor's garment in pledge, you shall return it to him before the sun sets; for that is his only clothing, the sole covering for his skin. In what shall he sleep?" (vs. 25–26).
12. Deut. 24:6.
13. *B.T.*, Berakhot, 33b; Megillah, 25a; Niddah, 16b.
14. Reading *wa* with Wolff and Ibn Tibbon (*we*), instead of *aw* (Kafih).
15. The text has the singular.
16. Lam. 3:38.
17. Lam. 3:39.
18. Lam. 3:40–41.
19. Maimonides does not specify what books he refers to.
20. Cf. *Guide*, I 73 (the sixth premise).
21. Literally: the six days of the Beginning.
22. Eccles. 1:9.
23. Literally: the six days of the Beginning.
24. *B.T.*, 'Avodah Zarah, 54b.
25. Gen. 3:22.
26. Reading *hādhihī al-shajarah* (Wolff), instead of *hādhā* (Kafih).
27. Gen. 3:22.
28. Gen. 15:13.

29. Deut. 31:16.
30. Isa. 66:3–4.
31. Exod. 14:4.
32. Literally: root.
33. Exod. 10:1.
34. Reading *lākin* with Wolff and Ibn Tibbon (*'ella'*); missing in Kafih.
35. Exod. 1:9–10.
36. Gen. 15:14.
37. Exod. 9:15–16.
38. I Kings 13:4.
39. Gen. 19:11.
40. Deut. 32:4.
41. Reading *al-ān* (Wolff), instead of *illā wa* (Kafih).
42. Exod. 9:16.
43. Deut. 2:30.
44. Reading *bi* as a copula.
45. It is unclear what Sihon's previous injustice was.
46. Isa. 6:10.
47. Literally: root.
48. I Kings 18:37.
49. Hosea 4:17.
50. Isa. 63:17.
51. Num. 14:15-16.
52. Isa. 63:17.
53. Malachi 2:17.
54. Malachi 3:14–15.
55. Malachi 3:18.
56. Literally: root.
57. Maimonides refers here to his explanation of the biblical verses that seem to deny human freedom.
58. *Mishnah,* Avot, I 13.
59. Reading *wa illā* (Wolff), instead of *awwalan* (Kafih).
60. Literally: root.
61. E.g., I Sam. 1:26; II Kings 2:2, 4, 6.
62. Gen. 42:15, 16.
63. E.g., I Sam. 20:3; II Kings 2:2, 4, 6.
64. Reading *wa ḥayātuh* with Wolff and Ibn Tibbon (*weḥayyaw*), instead of *wa 'ilmuh* (Kafih).
65. Maimonides apparently means that the adversaries referred to earlier died without ever having grasped the true meaning of God's knowledge.
66. Job 11:7.

III

ON THE MANAGEMENT OF HEALTH

This work was written in response to a letter from Saladin's son, al-Afḍal, who ruled Egypt for a short period of time. He had written to Maimonides complaining about a variety of bodily and emotional ailments, including constipation and indigestion as well as "bad thoughts," general anxiety, and the fear of death.

The letter to al-Afḍal, known as *On the Management of Health,* is divided into four chapters. After giving him some general medical advice, Maimonides discusses the treatment for al-Afḍal's particular illness in Chapter Three. In the first part of that chapter, which is not reproduced here, he prescribes remedies for al-Afḍal's physical ills. The rest of Chapter Three, which is translated below, deals with healing the diseases of the soul.

ON THE MANAGEMENT OF HEALTH

CHAPTER THREE

. . . It is known to our sovereign, may God prolong his days, that the passions of the soul greatly alter the body in ways obvious[1] to any observer. Consider a man with a powerful build, booming voice, and radiant face. If he were suddenly to receive news which greatly saddened him, in that instant you would see[2] his complexion become pale, the radiance of his face fade, his bearing slacken, and his voice drop. Even if he were to struggle to raise his voice, he would not be able to. His strength would wane, he might tremble because of weakness, his pulse would diminish, his eyes would become hollow, his lids would become too heavy to move, his skin would turn cold, and his appetite would subside. The cause of all of these effects would be the natural heat and the blood withdrawing deeper into the body. Conversely, consider an individual with a weak body, pale complexion, and feeble voice. If he were notified about something which greatly delighted him, you would see[3] his body become strong, his voice rise, his face brighten, his movements quicken, his pulse increase, his skin warm up, and joy and delight become so apparent that he would not be able to conceal them. The cause[4] of all of these effects would be the movement of the natural heat and the blood toward the surface of the body.

The characteristics of the fearful, anxious person and of the confident, relaxed person are known; similarly, the characteristics of the vanquished[5] and of the victorious are obvious. Whoever is vanquished[5] can hardly see anything[6] because his visual spirit is diminished and dissipated. However, the vision of the victorious person increases in such a massive way that the light of the atmosphere appears to have increased and grown. This is so obvious that it is not necessary to dwell on it.

For this reason physicians have recommended constant concern for, and awareness about, the soul's movements, as well as concern for putting them into equilibrium at the time of health and sickness—giving no other treatment precedence in any way. The physician should desire that every sick person and every healthy person be constantly cheerful[7] and relieved of the passions of the soul causing[8] depression.[9] In this way the health of the healthy will endure. This is foremost in curing every sick person, especially those whose sickness pertains to the soul—like those with hypochondria and morbid melancholia. Indeed, concern about the soul's movements ought to be strongest for these people, as well as for anyone overwhelmed by worry, obsessive thoughts, apprehension about things not[10] such as to produce apprehension, or anyone who is only slightly cheerful about cheerful things. For all of these people, the skillful physician should place nothing ahead of improving the condition of their souls by removing these passions.

However, insofar as he is a physician, the physician ought not to expect his art to provide knowledge of how to remove these passions. Indeed, this understanding is acquired from practical philosophy and from the admonitions and disciplines of the Law. For just as the philosophers have composed books about the various sciences, so too have they composed many books about improving moral habits and disciplining the soul to acquire the moral virtues so that only good actions stem from it. They warn[11] against the moral imperfections and teach every man who finds one of these moral habits in his soul the way to eradicate it so that the state of character leading to all evil actions disappears. Similarly, the disciplines of the Law, admonitions, maxims taken from the prophets (may peace be upon them) or from their followers, and knowledge of their virtuous lives improve the moral habits of the soul so that it obtains virtuous dispositions and only good actions stem from it.

Therefore you[12] find these[13] passions have a very great influence only on those individuals having no knowledge of philosophic ethics[14] or the disciplines and admonitions of the Law—such as youths, women, and foolish men. For due to the excessive tenderness of their souls, these people become anxious and despair. If harm touches them and one of the calamities of this world befalls them, you[15] find that their anxiety increases and that they cry out, weep, slap their cheeks, and beat their breasts. Sometimes the misfortunes[16] become so great in their eyes that one of them dies, either immediately or after a while, due to the worry and grief which overwhelm him. Similarly, if these individuals obtain one of the goods of this world, their joy thereby increases. Due to their souls being poorly disciplined, such individuals suppose that they have obtained a very great good, and their wonder and exultation[17] greatly magnify what they have obtained. Because of that, they are greatly moved and their laughter and frivolity increase to the point that some of them die from excessive joy. This is due to exhaustion of the spirit from the intensity of its suddenly tending to be outside of itself, as Galen mentioned. The cause of all this is the soul's excessive tenderness and its ignorance of the truth of things.

Now it is persons trained in philosophic ethics[18] or in the disciplines and admonitions of the Law whose souls acquire courage. These are the truly courageous; their souls[19] are only swayed and affected[20] in the slightest possible way. The more training an individual has, the less he is affected[21] by either of the two conditions—I mean, the condition of prosperity or of adversity. Even if he obtains one of the greater goods of this world, which are the ones the philosophers call presumed goods, he is not moved by that; nor do those goods[22] become great in his eyes. Similarly, if one of the greater evils of this world befalls him, which are the ones the philosophers call presumed evils, he does not become anxious nor despair, but endures it nobly.

A man acquires this disposition in his soul by considering the truth of things and by knowing the nature of existence. Even if a man possessed the greatest good of this world during his whole life, it would be very insignificant, because[23] it is a perishable thing and because man, like all the other kinds of animals, must die.[24] Similarly, if the greatest evil of this world is contrasted with death, which is inevitable, that evil is undoubtedly inferior to death. Therefore one should be less affected by that evil, since it is inferior to what is inevitable.

It is fitting that the philosophers called the goods and evils of this world, presumed goods and presumed evils. Indeed, how many of those goods are presumed to be good while being in truth evil, and how many of those evils are presumed to be evil while being in truth good? Again, how vast an amount of money and how many vain possessions has a man acquired which caused the corruption of his body, the degeneration of his soul through moral imperfections, the shortening of his life, his drawing away from God (may He be exalted), and separation between him and his Creator? Does that not give him everlasting misery?[25] Moreover, how much money has been stolen from a man or how many possessions wrested away which caused the improvement of his body, the ennobling of his soul with moral virtues, the lengthening of his life, and his coming closer to his Creator by devoting himself to His worship? Does that not give him everlasting happiness?[26]

Now the servant[27] could speak about the length or shortness of life only by relying upon the opinion of the physicians, the philosophers, and some of the adherents of the religious laws prior to Islam. In sum, most of what the multitude presumes to be happiness is in truth misery, while most of what it presumes to be misery is in truth happiness.

It is not the purpose of this treatise to explain the truth of these matters, to comment on them, and to teach the ways to them. Much has already been composed concerning this in every age and by every wise nation which has studied the sciences. The servant only offered this advice as an indication[28] of how to accustom the soul to diminish the passions[29] by studying books on ethics,[30] the disciplines of the Law, the admonitions, and the maxims spoken by intelligent men. In that way the soul will be strengthened and will see the true as true and the false as false. Thus the passions will diminish, [obsessive] thoughts will disappear, apprehension will be removed, and the soul will be cheerful in whatever condition a man happens to be.

Here[31] is a very good thing to reflect upon. By it, bad thoughts, worries, and griefs are diminished. Sometimes they can even be completely destroyed, if a man holds this reflection foremost in his mind. Namely, whenever a man thinks about something that distresses him, and worry, grief, or sadness crop up in him, it can be due only to one of two things: either he is thinking about a matter that has already taken place, like someone who thinks about something that happened to him, such as the loss of his money, or about the death of someone dear to him; or else he is thinking about matters he expects and whose advent he dreads, like someone who thinks and talks about the advent of any disaster he expects. Now intellectual reflection teaches that thinking about what has taken place and has happened is of no benefit at all, and that sadness and grief about matters that have passed and gone are due to faulty understanding.[32] There is no difference between a man's being grieved because of the loss of his money or similar things and his being grieved because he is a man and not an angel or a planet, or similar thinking about impossible things.

On the basis of this reflection, acts of thinking leading to depression about something that is expected to come to pass in the future ought also to be abandoned. That is because everything that a man expects is within the realm of possibility: it may take place or it may not take place. Hence, just as he becomes distressed and grieves lest what he expects occur, so too he ought to delight his soul with anticipation and hope that perhaps the opposite of what he expects will take place. After all, the expected matter and its opposite are both possible. . . .

NOTES

1. Omitting *bayyinah* with JTS and BN.
2. Reading *tarāh* (JTS), instead of *yarāh* (Kroner) or *tar* (BN).
3. Reading *tarāh* (JTS and BN), instead of *yarāh* (Kroner).
4. Reading *wa 'illah* (BN), instead of *'alaih* (Kroner) or *'illah* (JTS).
5. Reading *al-munhazim* (JTS and BN), instead of *al-munharim* (Kroner).
6. Reading *shai'* (JTS and BN), instead of *siyyamā* (Kroner).
7. Literally: cheerful of soul. The word translated as "cheerful" (*munbasiṭ*) connotes being expansive. Cf. *C.M.*, Eight Chapters, V, *supra*, p. 77 and notes seven and eight *ad loc.*
8. Reading *al-mūjibah* (JTS and BN), instead of *al-mūḥiyyah* (Kroner)
9. Literally: constriction of the soul.
10. Reading *lam yakun* on basis of *lam yakūn* (JTS), instead of *yumkin* (Kroner) or *yakūn* (BN).
11. Reading *yuḥadhdhirūn* (JTS and BN), instead of *yuḥaddirūn* (Kroner).
12. Reading *tajid* (JTS and BN), instead of *najid* (Kroner).
13. Reading *hādhīhī* (JTS and BN); omitted by Kroner.
14. Literally: philosophical moral habits.
15. See note twelve, *supra*.
16. Reading *al-maṣā'ib* (BN) instead of *al-maṣāb* (Kroner and JTS).
17. Reading *ghibṭatuh* (JTS), instead of *'atanuh* (Kroner and BN).
18. Literally: philosophical moral habits.
19. Omitting *ḥattā* (JTS and BN).
20. Reading *tanfa'il* (JTS and BN), instead of *tatafa"l* (Kroner).
21. Reading *infi'āl* (JTS and BN), instead of *tafa"al* (Kroner).
22. Reading *tilka al-khairāt* (JTS and BN), instead of *tilka* (Kroner).
23. Reading *idh huw* (JTS), instead of *wa huw* (Kroner and BN).
24. Reading *wa inna al-insān yamūt* (BN), instead of *wa mā li al-insān li yamūt* (Kroner and JTS).
25. Reading *al-shaqāwah* (JTS and BN), instead of *li al-shaqāwah* (Kroner).
26. Reading *al-sa'ādah* (JTS and BN), instead of *li al-sa'ādah* (Kroner).
27. That is, Maimonides.
28. Reading *li al-tanbīh* (JTS), instead of *bi al-tanbīh* (BN) or *al-tabyīn* (Kroner).
29. Reading *al-infi'ālāt* (JTS), instead of *al-infi'āl* (Kroner and BN).
30. Literally: moral habits.
31. Reading *wa hunā* (JTS and BN), instead of *wa hādhā* (Kroner).
32. Reading *nāqiṣīy al-taṣawwur* (JTS and BN), instead of *al-nāqiṣīy al-taṣawwur* (Kroner).

IV

LETTER TO JOSEPH

Maimonides wrote this letter to his favorite disciple, Joseph ben Judah, to whom the *Guide of the Perplexed* was dedicated. While in Baghdad Joseph had become embroiled in a bitter controversy with Samuel ben Ali, the Gaon of Baghdad, and with Samuel's son-in-law, Zechariah, who held a high office (*Av Bet Din*) at Samuel's court of law. Joseph had aroused Samuel's enmity by being instrumental in thwarting the latter's attempt to control the office of the Exilarch. Since Joseph wished to open a school in Baghdad and to teach Maimonides' Code there, the worth of the Code was another point of contention between Joseph and Samuel.

In the background of the letter lies the struggle between the "religious" leader, Samuel ben Ali, and the "secular" leader, the Exilarch. The question at stake is roughly comparable to the issue of Church versus State in the Christian world. Maimonides supported the independence of the Exilarchate against Samuel's plans to make the Exilarch his own puppet. Samuel's authority extended primarily over the Jewish legal system in Babylonia, while the Exilarch, besides his power to appoint judges in certain kinds of cases, could compel the acceptance of legal decisions among Jews anywhere in the world. Maimonides conceived of the Exilarch as being like the King of the Jews in Exile (*M.T.*, Laws Concerning the Sanhedrin, IV 13–14). His support of the Exilarchate resulted in a continued division of authority between the "secular" and "religious" leadership. The advantage of such a division is suggested by Maimonides' observation in the letter that "when religion is joined to [political] authority, piety disappears (#15)."

The unity of the letter has been questioned by some modern scholars, who claim that parts of it were written at different times and later combined by a scribe. David Baneth, who edited the Arabic text, argues for the unity of the letter. It is here presented as a single whole, without our intending to take sides in this dispute. The numbers in square brackets divide the letter into sections on the basis of Baneth's edition; they are not in the original text. The passages in diamond brackets are based upon a medieval Hebrew translation, which is used to fill lacunae in the Arabic text.

LETTER TO JOSEPH

[1] <By my belief in the Torah of our master Moses, my son[1] should know that I do not doubt anything you mentioned in your letter. I am certain things were truly like that. However, my moral habits are different from those of my son.> I[2] am very indulgent about what is due to me, whereas my son is unable to patiently forbear. In addition to what[3] thought dictates, age and experience have disciplined me.

[2] Know that I did not compose this *compilation*[4] in order to become preeminent among Jews nor to become famous. Thus I greatly regret that the purpose for which I composed it is disputed. God knows I composed it first of all for myself, to free myself from the [kind of] investigation and inquiry it requires, and also for the period of my old age. And [I composed it] for the sake of God, may He be exalted. Indeed, by God, *I have been very zealous for the Lord, God of Israel.*[5] I saw a religious community without a true law code and without correct and precise opinions, and so I did what I did purely for the sake of God. This is one consideration.

[3] A second consideration: While composing it I knew very well that it would fall into the hands of a wicked, envious man, who would debase its good qualities and pretend it is unnecessary or defective; or [it would fall] into the hands of an ignorant, foolish man who, not recognizing the value of what I have accomplished, would think it is of little benefit; or [it would fall] into the hands of a confused, bewildered beginner, for whom some of the passages in it would be too difficult, either because he does not know the principle[6] behind them or because his mind is incapable of grasping the precision with which they have been formulated; or [it would fall] into the hands of a dense, inflexible, devout person, who would attack what it contains about the principles of belief.[7] These people are in the majority. And [I knew] that it would [also] undoubtedly reach *the remnant who are called by the Lord,*[8] just and equitable men with excellent minds, who would recognize the value of what we have accomplished. You are the foremost among them. If no one besides you had come to me during my lifetime, that would have been enough. But in addition, letters have reached me from the *wise men of France* and from others,

with all of their signatures. They marvel at what has been accomplished and request the rest of it. It has already spread to the outer limit of civilization.

I refer only to my own time in all that I have described to you concerning those who do not accept it the way it deserves to be accepted. In the course of time, when envy and the quest for domination pass away, *all the sons of Israel* will be content with it alone and everything else will undoubtedly fall into disuse.[9] That is, except for someone who seeks something to occupy himself with for his whole life, without ever finishing it. Here, then, is another consideration; it shows that nothing happened[10] to me that I did not anticipate.

[4] A third consideration is that this compilation is not comparable, God forbid, to the *Torah,* which is truly the guide for mankind. Nor does it reach the level of the speech of the prophets. Still, only some people have followed it [the *Mishneh Torah*], while others have turned away from it. Ignorance about the value of this compilation is not more serious than all the ignorance that exists about divine things, let alone other things. If a man makes up his mind to become angry and vexed with everyone who is ignorant of some truth or who stubbornly contends against a certainty or single-mindedly follows some whim, he will undoubtedly pass *all of his days in pain and raging with anger.*[11] This ought not to happen.

[5] A fourth consideration: We shall describe some of my moral habits to you, even though you have come into contact with all of them. Know that here in the city with me there is a group of people who have no fame in the city, no standing, and no power. They are so afflicted with haughtiness and envy that they do not study this great compilation. They have not even looked at it yet so that no one might say: "This man is in a position to profit from the discourse of someone else and is therefore inferior to him in knowledge." They are mindful of the opinion of the common people in this matter and are forever *like a blind man groping in the darkness.*[12]

[6] How could my son not know that such moral habits would be found in someone brought up from his childhood to believe that no one like him exists in his generation?[13] Moreover, he has been encouraged [in that belief] by his old age, standing, ancestry, and by the absence of discerning men in

that area. His need of the people is such that he implants in their souls the abominable concoction that all of the people should seek to know about every matter coming from the *judicial academy*[14] or every honorific title it confers—besides those foolish things that naturally occur to them. How could my son imagine that he would reach such a level of recognition of the truth that he would admit[15] his incompetence and *uproot his honor as well as the honor of his father's house?*[16] This would not be done by someone like him or even by someone more perfect than he.

I am certain that to the extent that my name becomes known there, the situation compels him, his followers, and whoever wants to have standing with the people to find fault with my compilation. They pretend that they are too perfect to need to study it. Instead, they criticize it. [They pretend] that if one of them wanted to, he could quickly compose something finer. If what were said required attacking my religious observance[17] and my actions, he would do that.

[7] By God, all of this does not pain me, my son, even if I were to witness it and it were done in my presence. On the contrary, I have spoken in a refined manner, and I have kept silent or replied, depending upon the circumstances, for [their] neglect of the truth is far more serious than this. I do not come to my own defense, because my own dignity and moral character lead me to ignore fools, not to triumph over them with my tongue.[18] *The Holy One, blessed be He, guards the dignity of an eager student.*[19] Because I am his father and teacher, my son is forgiven for not being able to patiently forbear. However, my heart aches over your pain and preoccupation with this. Were you—God willing—to teach, enlighten, and instruct someone who is able to understand, and were you to reveal its[20] good qualities and to acquaint the people with it, that would be more worthy of you and me than engaging in controversy with these two.[21]

[8] As for this *Master Zechariah*,[22] he is a very foolish man. He has studied by himself and toiled over those *investigations and commentaries*.[23] He supposes himself to be unique in his time and to have already reached the highest perfection. <My esteemed son knows, by the living God, that my evaluation of the great wise men of Israel is based on my determining the

rank they deserve according to their own words. It was they who said: "The work of Abayya and Rabba is a small thing."[24] If this is a small thing in my sight>, why should I pay attention to a truly miserable old man, who is ignorant of everything and whom I view *indeed as an infant one day old?* Still, he is forgiven due to his ignorance.

[9] This jibberish which he jabbers concerning the *Commentary on the Mishnah* is all because I corrected some passages in it. *The Creator of everything* knows that I was in error about most of them because I followed the *Gaonim, may their memory be blessed,* such as *our master Nissim* in *The Revelation of Secrets* and *Rav Ḥefetz, may his memory be blessed,* in the Book of the *Commandments,* and others whom I am reluctant to mention.[25] Even if I myself have been mistaken, I do not claim that I reached my final perfection right from the beginning, nor that I have never erred. On the contrary, whenever a defect has become clear to me, I have always removed it from wherever it was found, whether in my compositions or my natural temperament.[26]

[10] A letter from him [Zechariah] expressing great humility and brimming with apology has reached me. I knew that the intent was to get a reply from me so that he could show the answer and boast about it without making known what he had written to me. The purpose of his letter was to glorify the head of the judicial academy as being unique in his generation, and the one whom the men of Baghdad wanted to appoint. When he [Zechariah] heard him [Samuel ben Ali] speak and saw him, he knew that it was not permitted to oppose him.[27] He was extremely verbose about this and said that the great men of the Maghrib[28] incessantly extolled the *judicial academy.* Then he requested that we support him [Samuel ben Ali].

[11] A second letter also came to me, this one from the head of the judicial academy. It described to me, among the rest of his virtues, the greatness of the aforementioned *Master Zechariah,* that his understanding is great and that *he knows four Orders of the Talmud by heart.* There was much more with this end in view. *They reciprocated with one another.*[29] I know the purpose of both these miserable men and that their intent is to receive a reply. Now a man cannot avoid being courteous in letters. One is unable to do away with civility in speaking—how much less so in letters. Thus, they would make this [the letter] public and

glorify themselves through it, without the people knowing what they had written. Because of that, I delayed answering them until now.

[12] The cause that made the first exchange of letters necessary is as follows. It is proper to demand a detailed account of the actions and words of someone like myself. They denounced me for recommending someone whose qualifications I know nothing about, someone who is a good-for-nothing. He [Samuel ben Ali] mentioned that every *disciple of the wise* is estranged from this *Exilarch*[30] and detests him. Therefore I had to justify myself. I explained that I had recommended him on the testimony of my disciple, [31] in whose religious observance[32] and knowledge I have complete confidence, and on the testimony of an elder from his city, namely, Abū al-Riḍā ibn Ṭibūn, whom I had asked about the religious observance[32] and conduct [of the candidate]. They praised him highly, and I thereupon recommended him. In the letter which I wrote to him [Samuel ben Ali], I included only this matter and the advice to put an end to the *controversy* and to be like a father to you. Indeed, your rank is not his, nor is his rank yours.

[13] <Because they told me that my son had reviled him, called him "a foolish old man" and spoken harshly about him, I wrote in the course of that letter: "Those who say such things are gossipmongers; he would not think it permissible to do something like that. In his letter, which is in my hands, he praises you and says that there is no one like you in Iraq." In this vein I wrote to him.> I was on my guard about everything [that I was about to do because of what][33] my son had advised. You know of my humility with everyone and that I put myself on the same level as the most insignificant person. However, I deviated from my moral habits in that letter because of your advice.

[14] What I wish from my esteemed, dear son—in accordance with your duty to God and to me—is that you not grind this man[34] into the ground. *If no wisdom is here, there is old age here.*[35] It is not acceptable for a young man to attack *an old man who is the head of a judicial academy.*[36] May God restrain you from humiliating someone who is great in the sight of the people. But more than that, I beseech you to treat as great anyone who is insignificant in the sight of the people.

[15] Do not let his speaking harshly about you in the letter publicized in *Israel* continue to distress you. Is anyone struck without crying out? Don't you know that you have greatly harmed him, threatened his splendor, and punctured his dignity?[37] Indeed, were it not for you, the *Exilarch* would have been in his hands like a pullet in the claws of a hawk. Moreover, he would have denounced him about the matter of the bill of divorce and other things and would have torn him apart. So do not expect that someone you have harmed will love you and thank you. Nor is there any need for you to say, "But where is religion?" No, because for this man and those like him among even greater men of former times, religion is nothing more than a way to avoid major sins, which is how the common people view it. They do not believe the duties of ethics[38] to be part of religion, nor are they as careful about what they say as men of perfect piety are. Now, most of these [aforementioned] religious men were in positions of [political] authority, and when religion is joined to [political] authority, piety disappears. Everyone cannot be expected to be *like Ḥanina ben Dosa and Pinḥas ben Yair*,[39] may peace be upon them. Nor should anyone not at that level be called irreligious.

[16] In sum, if you are indeed my disciple, I want you to train yourself to follow my moral habits. The most noble conduct for you is to be reviled without reviling in turn and without letting your words get away from you. Above all, show the fear of God in your words, and let the criticism of intelligent and religious men be last of all. Make your goal with this man never to attack him about anything—if you are unable to achieve a reconciliation with him. A man is able to reply, criticize, and oppose [others] in a refined and friendly way. Do not depart from my advice in any respect.

[17] I have already written the letter you asked me to write to the *Exilarch*. His letter has reached me, and I have had it read aloud in my house while standing up. Everybody in Fustat,[40] *from young to old,* was in the house, for there was a *circumcision* and it was *Sukkoth.* They all stood up when I did, and it was a great day for him.[41] *R. Samuel, the teacher,* read it. All the elders of the community were on the dais, from right to left. Is there anything more you can ask of me?

I wrote to the head of the judicial academy that if I had

known about the *controversy* and dispute there, I would not have stepped in among them. However, I had already acted, *and the horn had already been heard in Yavneh.*[42] I explained that to him and informed him that it was impossible to turn things back. My esteemed son should let the head of the judicial academy know what I have done. You should know that I will not reply to him until I receive a letter from my son clarifying these matters I am speaking about—after you have thoroughly investigated them.

[18] As for the treatise,[43] I am amazed at my son. Why did he send it to me—so that I would thereby learn of the paucity of his [Samuel ben Ali's] knowledge? What, do you suppose that I consider him or someone greater than he to know anything? As far as I am concerned, his limits are those of every preacher: he stumbles around the way others stumble around. God knows, I have been amazed at how he would know enough to say these foolish things, ridiculous and disgraceful as they are. But the fluency of the miserable man! If he were content[44] to give a proof taken from *the hundred blessings and the blessing by whoever sees the graves of Israel,*[45] that would be more appropriate for him than to discuss the soul and the opinions of the philosophers. However, because he equates himself with someone greater than he is, he raves even more than this. He has undoubtedly transmitted the raving of someone else.[46]

[19] A letter from Yemen similar to what was mentioned has reached me, and I answered them. However, those people confused *the world-to-come* with *the days of the messiah,* in spite of the explanation we gave in *Pereq Heleq.*[47] There we were very explicit and gave a complete enumeration of those *who have no portion in the world-to-come,* among whom is *the one who denies the resurrection of the dead.*[48] How could anyone with a sound intellect imagine that this is a principle[49] that someone who believes in the *religion of Israel* would not believe in, especially since it is well known and obvious? It is astonishing that those who asked the question,[50] the one who responded,[51] and even you say we ought not to interpret the verses of the *Bible* referring to the *resurrection of the dead.* Who should interpret that? Who should undertake this? In sum, I shall compose a treatise about that, and it will reach you shortly in my own handwriting.

[20] I have already sent you six fascicles of the *Guide*[52] which I took back from someone else. They complete the first part. I am uncertain whether I sent you the introduction I had joined to them. Therefore I am sending it to you now. None other than the *pious judge,* Abū al-Muhāsan, copied them. Guard them very closely and do not lose them so that I am not harmed by *the Gentiles and the many wicked men of Israel.*

[21] As for what you mentioned about going to Baghdad, I have already given you permission to open *a house of study* and to teach and give legal opinions, while you persevere in defending the *compilation.*[53] However, I am afraid that you will be continually plagued by evils from them,[54] so that in the end only evil will be the result. Also, if you are completely attached to teaching, your business will suffer. I do not advise taking money from them. So far as I am concerned, one dirhem as a wage for tailoring, carpentry, or weaving is preferable to the *income of the Exilarch.*[55] If you work with them, you will be financially ruined; if you take money from them, you will be viewed with contempt. In my opinion, you should apply your labors to business and the study of medicine, along with occupying yourself with the *study of* the true *Torah.* Teach only the *laws* of the *Master,*[56] *may his memory be blessed,* and compare them with the *compilation.*[57] If you[58] find a contradiction, you will know that reflection on the *Talmud* leads to that; so search for the passages. If you spend your time on the *commentaries,* the *explanations* of the intricate problems of the *Gemara,*[59] and those matters from which we have been relieved, time will be wasted and the benefit will diminish. Whatever you decide, let me know. May God guide you along the best paths.

[22] I tell you I have already acquired a very great reputation in medicine among the distinguished men—such as the Supreme Judge, the Princes, the court of al-Fāḍil,[60] and other leaders of the country—from whom one obtains nothing.[61] As for the common people, I have been elevated above them and they have no access to me, due to my continually spending my days in Cairo[62] visiting the sick.[63] When I get to Fustat, my goal during the rest of the day and night is to be able to peruse the medical books for what I need. You know how extensive and difficult this art is for someone religious and precise, who does not want to say anything unless he knows the proof for it,

where it is mentioned, and the reasoning behind it. This is why I do not find a single hour to study anything pertaining to the Law and I study only on the Sabbath. Nor do we find time to study anything of the other sciences. I have suffered a great deal on this account. Recently I received everything that Averroes composed on the books of Aristotle, except *On Sensation and the Sensible.* I think that he is extraordinarily correct, but I have not yet found time to go over all of his books.

[23] Do not deprive me of your letters, for I have no more intimate companion than they. When Ibn al-Mashāṭ arrives from India,[64] give him an account of what I have told you. All of our friends send you greetings. Abū al-Maʿālī[65] the elder, his brother and our son Abū al-Riḍā,[66] and everyone in my household—the free men and the servants—rejoice in hearing good news about you, God knows. With one voice they pray for a reunion with you, in accord with their wish and yours. Give my best greetings to your father-in-law, *R. Josiah,* the venerable old man, the pious, faithful, and trustworthy *judge, the glory of our holy, eminent scholars, the diligent student, the splendor of the priests and their strength, may his Rock and Redeemer guard him.* Also, convey my best greetings to his son, may God increase his delight in him. *May he see offspring; may his days be long.*[67] In spite of the express legal prohibition, *never ask about the peace [or welfare] of a woman,*[68] a prayer is not forbidden. *May you be at peace and may your home be at peace.*[69] *At the appointed time, may Sarah have a son.*[70] *May your peace increase and be great, in accord with your wish and the wish of the writer,*

Moses son of R. Maimon.

At the beginning of the month of *Marḥeshvon, 1191.*[71]

NOTES

1. Maimonides refers affectionately to Joseph ben Judah in the letter as his son (or as "the son" in the Arabic text, translated as "my son"). According to Jewish tradition, a student is like the teacher's son; the teacher needs "to watch over his students and love them, for they are the sons who give pleasure in this world and for the world-to-come" (*M.T.*, Laws of the Study of Torah, V 12; cf. I 2).
2. We have omitted the command "know that," which precedes the pronoun "I." In the next sentence, we have omitted "he said," which precedes "in addition," and also the words, "he said to him," at the beginning of the next paragraph. We thus agree with Baneth's interpretation that the omitted words were not part of the original text.
3. Reading *ilā mā* (ed. Simonson), instead of *lī mā*.
4. The *Mishneh Torah*.
5. I Kings 19:10. The original verse reads: "I have been very zealous for the Lord, God of hosts."
6. Literally: root.
7. Literally: roots of beliefs.
8. Joel 3:5.
9. According to the Introduction to the *Mishneh Torah*, there is no need to study any other work on the Oral Law besides the *Mishneh Torah* (ed. Hyamson, p. 4b).
10. Reading *yatra'*, instead of *yatrā*.
11. Eccles. 2:23.
12. Deut. 28:29.
13. The reference is to Samuel ben Ali, the head of the Baghdad judiciary. The abrupt change from the subject of the preceding paragraph could be explained as due either to a faulty transmission of the original text or to the transcribing of several letters on a single manuscript.
14. *Yeshivah*, which refers to an assembly whose purpose is to render legal decisions. At that time it did not have the later meaning of a center for the study of the *Talmud*.
15. Reading *ya'tarif*, instead of *yata'arraf*.
16. *B.T.*, Horayot, 14a.
17. Literally: religion. The Arabic word is *dīn*, which refers to beliefs as well as practices.
18. More literally: I do not defend my soul, because my soul's nobility and my character lead me to ignore fools, not to triumph over them with my tongue.
19. *B.T.*, Berakhot, 19a.
20. The *Mishneh Torah*.
21. Samuel ben Ali and Zechariah.

22. Samuel ben Ali's son-in-law, who was a high official (*Av Bet Din*) at Samuel's law court in Baghdad.
23. The study of the *Talmud* and its commentaries.
24. Cf. *B.T.*, Sukkah, 28a, where the "small thing," the *Talmud,* is contrasted with a "great thing," the Account of the Chariot, which Maimonides identifies as divine science or metaphysics (*M.T.*, Laws of the Foundations of the Torah, IV 13; *Guide,* Introduction [3b]).
25. Or: whose memory is dear to us.
26. Literally: my nature. The word translated as "composition" (*wad'*) also connotes "convention," so that the sentence alludes both to what is by convention and what is by nature.
27. Zechariah had originally come from Aleppo to Baghdad in order to study with Samuel ben Ali. The latter's opponents attempted to enlist his support, for Zechariah was already a recognized scholar, but he joined Samuel's judiciary and after a while was appointed to the position of *Av Bet Din.* See S. Assaf, "Qovetz shel Iggrot R. Shmuel ben Ali Uvnei Doro," *Tarbiz,* I, 1, (Oct. 1929), pp. 107–108; I, 2 (Jan. 1930), p. 61.
28. The region encompassing northwestern Africa and Moorish Spain.
29. *Mishnah,* Demai, IV 6.
30. Samuel of Mosul.
31. Presumably Joseph ben Judah.
32. Literally: religion. See note seventeen.
33. The brackets contain the reading of Baneth, who reconstructed the text on the basis of a medieval Hebrew translation.
34. Reading *al-rajul,* instead of *al-rajūl.*
35. Cf. *B.T.*, Berakhot, 39a, which reads: "If no wisdom is here, is not old age here?"
36. *B.T.*, Yoma, 28b.
37. Literally: destroyed his arrows.
38. Or: moral habits.
39. Two talmudic sages renowned for their piety.
40. Literally: "Old Cairo" (*Maṣr*) from *Maṣr al-Fusṭāṭ,* which was on the outskirts of the Fatimid capitol, Cairo. Even though Fustat had been more populous and prosperous than Cairo at one point, by the time of Maimonides its decline had begun.
41. On this occasion, the Exilarch was publicly endorsed by Maimonides as well as by the important Jewish community of Fustat. Maimonides strongly supported the office of the Exilarchate, regarding the Exilarchs as being in the stead of kings. *M.T.*, Laws Concerning the Sanhedrin, IV 13–14; *C.M.*, Bekhorot, IV 4.
42. *B.T.*, Rosh Hashanah, 29b.
43. The treatise of Samuel ben Ali in which he replied to a question from Yemen concerning the resurrection of the dead, and attacked the position of Maimonides on this subject. Maimonides'

own *Treatise on the Resurrection of the Dead* was in response to this attack.

44. Following Baneth's suggestion and reading *iqtaṣar,* instead of *istaqar.*

45. Among the one hundred blessings that a Jew is required to recite each day, two refer to the resurrection of the dead. There is a separate blessing to be recited when the graves of Jews are seen, and this blessing concludes with a reference to the resurrection of the dead (*B.T.,* Berakhot, 58b).

46. The reference is apparently to Saadia, who seems to have influenced the view of Samuel ben Ali concerning the resurrection of the dead.

47. The world-to-come is achieved through the permanent preservation of the intellect and hence can be attained at any time. See the selection from *Pereq Ḥeleq* translated below.

48. Among the thirteen principles ("foundations") enumerated in *Pereq Ḥeleq* is the affirmation of the resurrection of the dead.

49. Literally: foundation.

50. The Yemenites.

51. Samuel ben Ali. See note forty-three.

52. Although this word is in Arabic, it is in italics here because it refers to the title of a book.

53. The *Mishneh Torah.*

54. Samuel ben Ali and his companions.

55. The communities under the jurisdiction of the Exilarch were obliged to pay taxes to him.

56. Alfasi (1013–1103), who was the author of an important code of Jewish law.

57. The *Mishneh Torah.*

58. The second person plural is used throughout this sentence to refer to Joseph and his students. The next sentence has the second person singular.

59. The *Gemara* is the main part of the *Talmud* and contains lengthy discussions of the laws set forth in the *Mishnah.*

60. The vizier of Saladin.

61. No fees were collected from such distinguished men, but presumably they gave Maimonides gifts for services rendered.

62. The caliphs and the military aristocracy lived in Cairo.

63. In a letter to Samuel ibn Tibbon, Maimonides gives a rather different account of his medical practice in Fustat. He says that when he returns from Cairo to Fustat in the afternoon, he finds his antechambers filled with patients, whom he attends until nightfall, and then collapses from exhaustion. Maimonides tells this to Ibn Tibbon in order to dissuade him from making a visit to Egypt. *Qovetz Teshuvot ha-Rambam,* ed. A. Lichtenberg (Leipzig: 1849), II 28a.

64. The words "and our friends" follow, but do not appear to be part of the original text. Cf. Baneth's note *ad loc.*
65. Maimonides' brother-in-law, who achieved renown as a scribe and secretary to Saladin's wife, the mother of al-Afdal.
66. The son of Abū al-Maʿālī. Maimonides refers to him affectionately as "our son."
67. Isa. 53:10.
68. *B.T.*, Kiddushin, 70b.
69. I Sam. 25:6. The rabbis refer to a man's wife as his "home."
70. Gen. 18:14.
71. This is apparently a scribal error and should read 1190. The *Treatise on the Resurrection of the Dead* was written in 1190 and, according to the letter (#19), it had not yet been written. See Baneth, p. 33.

V

GUIDE OF THE PERPLEXED

Addressed to Joseph ben Judah and others like him, the *Guide* is intended to resolve the perplexity that philosophy poses for a student of the Law. Since the validity of the Law appears to be questioned by philosophy, the *Guide* contains a defense of the Law, including its practical purposes. Though largely speculative in character, the *Guide* therefore touches upon ethical matters. It is true that Maimonides accepts the Aristotelian distinction between the theoretical and practical sciences (*Logic*, XIV). One might therefore think that a work whose intention is avowedly speculative would exclude practical questions from its purview. The *Guide* is not, however, concerned with the theoretical sciences as such, but with the theoretical foundations of the Law, the "true science of the Law." Knowledge of the foundations of the Law cuts across the distinction between the theoretical and practical spheres.

The following selections are reprinted, with minor changes, from the translation by Shlomo Pines (Chicago: University of Chicago Press, 1963), which was based on the Arabic text established by S. Munk (1856-66) and edited by I. Joel (1930). The numbers in brackets in the body of the text refer to the pagination of Munk's edition.

GUIDE OF THE PERPLEXED

PART I

Chapter 2

Years ago a learned man propounded as a challenge to me a curious objection. It behooves us now to consider this objection and our reply invalidating it. However, before mentioning this objection and its invalidation, I shall make the following statement. Every Hebrew knew that the term *Elohim* is equivocal, designating the deity, the angels, and the rulers governing the cities. *Onqelos the Proselyte,* peace be on him, has made it clear, and [13b] his clarification is correct, that in the dictum of Scripture, *And you shall be as Elohim, knowing good and evil,*[1] the last sense is intended. For he has translated: *And you shall be as rulers.* After thus having set forth the equivocality of this term, we shall begin to expound the objection.

This is what the objector said: It is manifest from the clear sense of the biblical text that the original purpose with regard to man was that he should be, as the other animals are, devoid of intellect, of thought, and of the capacity to distinguish between good and evil. However, when he disobeyed, his disobedience procured for him as its necessary consequence the great perfection peculiar to man, namely, his having the capacity that exists in us to make this distinction. Now this capacity is the noblest of the characteristics[2] existing in us; it is in virtue of it that we are constituted as substances. It is surely a thing to be wondered at that man's punishment for his disobedience should consist in his being granted a perfection that he did not possess before, namely, the intellect. This is like the story told by somebody that a certain man from among the people disobeyed and committed great crimes, and in consequence was made to undergo a metamorphosis,[3] becoming a star in heaven. This was the intent and the meaning of the objection, though it was not literally as we have put it.

Hear now the intent of our reply. We said: O you who engage in theoretical speculation using the first notions that may occur to you and come to your mind and who consider withal that you understand a book that is the guide of the first and the last men while glancing through it as you would glance through a historical work or a piece of poetry—when, in some of your hours of leisure, you leave off drinking and copulating: collect yourself and reflect, for things are not as you thought following the first notion that occurred to you, but rather as is made clear through reflection upon the following speech.[4] For the intellect that God made overflow unto man and that is the latter's ultimate perfection, was that which *Adam* had been provided with before he disobeyed. It was because of this that it was said of him that he was created *in the image of God and in His likeness.* It was likewise on account of it that he was addressed by God and given commandments, as it says: *And the Lord* [14a] *God commanded, and so on.*[5] For commandments are not given to beasts and beings devoid of intellect. Through the intellect one distinguishes between truth and falsehood, and that was found in [Adam] in its perfection and integrity. Base and noble,[6] on the other hand, belong to the generally accepted opinions,[7] not the intelligibles. For one does not say: it is noble that heaven is spherical, and it is base that the earth is flat; rather one says true and false [with regard to these assertions]. Similarly one expresses in our language the notions of truth and falsehood by means of the terms *emeth* and *sheqer,* and those of noble and base by means of the terms *ṭov* and *ra'.*[8] Now man in virtue of his intellect knows *truth* from *falsehood*; and this holds good for all intelligible things. Accordingly when man was in his most perfect and excellent state, in accordance with his inborn disposition and possessed his intellectual cognitions—because of which it is said of him: *You have made him but little lower than Elohim*[9]—he had no faculty that was engaged in any way with considering generally accepted opinions, and he did not apprehend them. So among these generally accepted things even that which is most manifestly base, namely, uncovering the genitals, was not base according to him, and he did not apprehend that it was base. However, when he disobeyed and inclined toward his imaginary desires and the pleasures of his corporeal senses— inasmuch as it is said: *that the tree was good for food and that it was a delight to the eyes*[10]—he was punished by being deprived of that intellectual apprehension. He therefore disobeyed the commandment that was imposed upon him on account of his intellect and, attaining the apprehension of generally accepted opinions, he became absorbed with considering things base or noble. Then he knew how great his loss was, what he had been deprived of, and upon what a state he had entered. Hence it is said: *And you shall be like Elohim knowing good and evil;*[11] and not: *knowing the false and the true,* or *apprehending the false and the true.* With regard to what is of necessity, there is no *good* and *evil* at all, but only the *false* and the *true.* Reflect on the dictum: *And the eyes of them both were opened, and they knew that they were naked.*[12] It is not said: *And the eyes of them both were opened,* [14b] *and they saw.* For what was seen previously was exactly that which was seen afterwards. There had been no membrane over the eye that was now removed, but rather he entered upon another state in which he considered as base things that he had not previously considered base. Know, moreover, that this expression, I mean, *to open,*[13] refers only to uncovering mental vision and in no respect means that the sense of sight has been newly acquired. Thus: *And God opened her eyes;*[14] *Then the eyes of the blind shall be opened;*[15] *Opening the ears, he hears not*[16]—which is analogous to the verse, *That have eyes to see and see not.*[17] Now concerning its saying with regard to *Adam—He changes his face and You send him forth*[18]—the interpretation and explanation of the verse are as follows: when the direction toward which man tended[19] changed, he was driven forth. For *panim*[20] is a term deriving from the verb *panoh [to turn],* since man turns his face toward the thing he wishes to take as his objective. The verse states accordingly that when man changed the direction toward which he tended and took as his objective the very thing a previous commandment had bidden him not to aim at, he was driven out of the *Garden of Eden.* This was the punishment corresponding to his disobedience; it was *measure for measure.* He had been given license to eat good things and to take pleasure in ease and tranquillity. When, however, as we have said, he became greedy, followed his pleasures and his imaginings, and ate what he had been forbidden to eat, he was deprived of everything and had to eat the meanest kinds of food, which he had not used as aliment before—and this only after toil and labor. As it says: *Thorns also and thistles shall it bring forth to you, and so on; In the sweat of your brow, and so on.*[21] And it explains and says: *And the Lord God sent him forth from the Garden of Eden, to till the ground.*[22] And God reduced him, with respect to his food and most of his circumstances, to the level of the beast. It says accordingly: *And you shall eat the grass of the field.*[23] And it also says in explanation of this story: *Adam,*[24] *unable to dwell in dignity, is like the beasts that speak not.*[25]

Praise be to the Master of the will whose aims and wisdom cannot be apprehended!

PART II

Chapter 33

It is clear to me that at the *Gathering at Mount Sinai,* not everything that reached *Moses* also reached all *Israel.* Speech was addressed to *Moses* alone; for this reason, in the whole *Decalogue* the second person singular is used, and he, peace be on him, went to the foot of the mountain and communicated to the people what he had heard. The text of the *Torah* reads: *I stood between the Lord and you at that time to declare unto you the word of the Lord.*[1] It also says: *Moses spoke, and God answered him by a voice.*[2] And it is explicitly said in the *Mekhilta*[3] that he repeated to them each and every *commandment* as he heard it. Again a text of the *Torah* reads: *That the people may hear when I speak with you, and so on.*[4] This is a proof that it was he who was spoken to and that they heard the great voice, but not the articulations of speech. About hearing [75a] this great voice, it says: *When you heard the voice.*[5] And it also says: *You heard the voice of words, but you saw no figure; only a voice.*[6] It does not say: *you heard the words.* Thus every time when their hearing words is mentioned, it is their hearing the *voice* that is meant, *Moses* being the one who heard words and reported them to them. This is the external meaning of the text of the *Torah* and of most of the dicta of the *sages, may their memory be blessed.* However, they also have a dictum formulated in several passages of the *Midrashim*[7] and also figuring in the *Talmud.* This is their dictum:[8] *They heard "I"*[9] *and "You shall not have"*[10] *from the mouth of the Force.*[11] They mean that these words reached them just as they reached *Moses our master* and that it was not *Moses our master* who communicated them to them. For these two principles,[12] I mean the existence of the deity and His being one, are apprehended by human speculation alone. Now with regard to everything that can be known by demonstration, the status of the prophet and that of everyone else who knows it are equal; there is no superiority of one over the other. Thus these two principles¹² are not known through prophecy alone. The text of the *Torah* says: *Unto you it was shown, and so on.*¹³ As for the other *commandments*, they belong to the class of generally accepted opinions and traditions, not to the class of intelligibles¹⁴. . . .

Chapter 40

It has been explained with utmost clarity that man is political by nature and that it is his nature to live in society. He is not like the other animals for which society is not a necessity. Because of the complex composition of this species¹—for, as you know, it is the last one to have been composed—there are many differences between the individuals belonging to it, so that you can hardly find two individuals who are alike in [85b] any one of the kinds of moral habits, except in a way similar to that in which their visible forms may be alike. The cause of this is the difference of the mixtures,² owing to which the various kinds of matter differ, and also the accidents that are a consequence of the form in question. For every natural form has certain distinctive accidents that are a consequence of it, those accidents being different from those which are a consequence of the matter. Nothing like this great difference between the various individuals is found among the other species of animals, in which the difference between individuals belonging to the same species is small, man being in this respect an exception. For you may find among us two individuals who seem, with regard to every moral habit, to belong to two different species. Thus you may find in an individual cruelty that reaches a point at which he kills the youngest of his sons in his great anger, whereas another individual is full of pity at the killing of a bug or any other insect, his soul being too tender for this. The same holds good for most accidents.

Now as the nature of the human species requires that there be those differences among the individuals belonging to it and as in addition society is a necessity for this nature, it is by no means possible that his society should be perfected except—

and this is necessarily so—through a ruler who gauges the actions of the individuals, perfecting that which is deficient and reducing that which is excessive, and who prescribes actions and moral habits that all of them must always practice in the same way, so that the natural diversity is hidden through the multiple points of conventional accord and so that the community becomes well ordered. Therefore I say that the Law, although it is not natural, has a connection with what is natural. It is part of the wisdom of the deity with regard to the permanence of this species—whose existence He has willed— that He put into its nature that individuals belonging to it should have the faculty of ruling. Among them there is the one to whom the aforementioned governance has been revealed by prophecy directly; i.e., the prophet or someone who lays down the nomos.[3] Among them there are also those who have the faculty to compel people to accomplish, observe, [86a] and actualize that which has been established by those two.[4] They are a sovereign who adopts the nomos in question, and someone claiming to be a prophet who adopts the Law of the prophet—either the whole of it or a portion. His adopting a portion and abandoning another portion may be due either to this being easier for him or to his wishing out of jealousy to make people fancy that those matters came to him through a prophetic revelation and that with regard to them he does not follow somebody else. For among the people there are men who admire a certain perfection, take pleasure in it, have a passion for it, and wish people to imagine that this perfection belongs to them, though they know that they possess no perfection. Thus you see that there are many who lay a claim to, and give out as their own, the poetry of someone else. This has also been done with regard to certain works of men of science and to particular points of many sciences. For an envious and lazy individual sometimes comes upon a thing invented by somebody else and claims that it was he who invented it. This has also happened with regard to the prophetic perfection. For we find people who laid a claim to prophecy and said things with regard to which there had never been at any time a prophetic revelation coming from God; thus, for instance, *Zedekiah, son of Chenaanah*.[5] And we find other people who laid a claim to prophecy and said things that God has indubitably said—I mean that had come through a prophetic revelation, but a prophetic revelation addressed to other people; thus, for instance, *Hananiah, son of Azzur.*[6] Accordingly these men give out as their own the prophetic revelation in question and adorn themselves with it. The knowledge and discernment of all this are very clear. I shall explain this to you so that the matter not be obscure to you and that you have a criterion by means of which you are able to distinguish between the rule[7] of nomoi that have been laid down, the rule[7] of the divine Law, and the rule[7] of those who take over something from the dicta of the prophets, raise a claim to it, and give it out as their own.

Concerning the nomoi with respect to which those who have laid them down have stated clearly that these are nomoi they have laid down by following their own thoughts, there is no need to adduce proofs for this, for with its being recognized by the adversary, no further evidence is needed. Accordingly I only want to give you knowledge concerning the ordinances[7] [86b] with regard to which the claim is made that they are prophetic; some of them are truly prophetic—I mean divine— while others are nomoi,[8] and others again are plagiarisms.

Accordingly if you find a Law the whole end of which and the whole purpose of the ruler thereof, who determined the actions required by it, are directed exclusively toward the ordering of the city[9] and of its circumstances and the abolition in it of injustice and oppression; and if in that Law attention is not at all directed toward speculative matters, no heed is given to the perfecting of the rational faculty, and no regard is accorded to opinions being correct or faulty—the whole purpose of that Law being, on the contrary, the arrangement, in whatever way this may be brought about, of the circumstances of people in their relations with one another and provision for their obtaining, in accordance with the opinion of that ruler, a certain something deemed to be happiness—you must know that that Law is a nomos[10] and that the man who laid it down belongs, as we have mentioned, to the third class, I mean to say to those who are perfect only in their imaginative faculty.

If, on the other hand, you find a Law all of whose ordinances are due to attention being paid, as was stated before, to the soundness of the body's condition and also to the soundness of belief—a Law that takes pains to inculcate correct opinions with regard to God, may He be exalted in the first place, and with regard to the angels, and that desires to make man wise, to give him understanding, and to awaken his attention, so that he should know the whole of that which exists in its true form— you must know that this guidance comes from Him, may He be exalted, and that this Law is divine.

It remains for you to know whether he who lays claim to such a guidance is a perfect man to whom a prophetic revelation of that guidance has been vouchsafed, or whether he is an individual who lays claim to these dicta, having plagiarized them. The way of putting this to a test is to consider the perfection of that individual, to examine his actions carefully, and to study his way of life. The strongest of the indications you should pay attention to is constituted by his renunciation of, and contempt for, the bodily pleasures, for this is the first of the degrees of the people of science and, all the more, of the prophets. In particular this holds good with regard to the sense [87a] that is a disgrace to us—as Aristotle has set forth[11]— and especially in what belongs to it with regard to the foulness of copulation. For this reason God has stigmatized through it everyone who lays a claim to prophecy, so that the truth will be made clear to those who seek it and they will not go astray and fall into error. Do you not see how *Zedekiah, son of Maaseiah, and Ahab, son of Kolaiah,* claimed prophecy, were followed by the people, and gave forth dicta deriving from a revelation that had come to others; and how they were plunged into the vileness of the pleasure of sexual intercourse so that they fornicated with the wives of their companions and followers so that God made them notorious, just as He disgraced others, and *the King of Babylon* burned them. As *Jeremiah* has set forth, saying: *And of them shall be taken up a curse by all the exiles of Judah that are in Babylon, saying: The Lord make you like Zedekiah and like Ahab, whom the King of Babylon roasted in the fire; because they have wrought vile deeds in Israel, and have committed adultery with their neighbors' wives, and have spoken words in My name falsely, which I commanded them not; but I am He that knows and am witness, says the Lord.*[12] Understand this intention.

PART III

Chapter 26

Just as there is disagreement among the men of speculation among the adherents of Law whether His works, may He be exalted, are consequent upon wisdom or upon the will alone without being intended toward any end at all, there is also the same disagreement among them regarding our laws, which He has given to us. Thus there are people who do not seek for them [57b] any cause at all, saying that all the laws are consequent upon the will alone. There are also people who say that every commandment and prohibition in these laws is consequent upon wisdom and aims at some end, and that all the laws have causes and were given in view of some utility. It is, however, the doctrine of all of us—both of the multitude and of the elite—that all the laws have a cause, though we are ignorant of the causes for some of them and we do not know the manner in which they conform to wisdom. With regard to this the texts of the Book are clear: *righteous statutes [huqqim] and judgments;*[1] *The judgments of the Lord are true, they are righteous altogether.*[2]

About the statutes designated as *huqqim*[3]—for instance those concerning the *mixed fabric, meat in milk,* and *the sending of the goat*[4]—[the sages], *may their memory be blessed,* make literally the following statement: *Things which I have prescribed for you, you have no permission to investigate. Satan criticizes them and the nations of the world argue against them.*[5] They are not believed by the multitude of the *sages* to be things for which there is no cause at all and for which one must not seek an end. For this would lead, according to what we have explained, to their being considered as frivolous actions. On the contrary, the multitude of the *sages* believe that there indubitably is a cause for them—I mean to say a useful end—but that it is hidden from us either because of the incapacity of our intellects or the deficiency of our knowledge. Consequently there is, in their opinion, a cause for all the *commandments;* I mean to say that any particular commandment or prohibition has a useful end. In the case of some of them, it is clear to us in what way they are useful—as in the case of the prohibition of killing and stealing. In the case of others, their utility is not clear—as in the case of the interdiction of the *first products*[6] [of trees] and of [sowing] *the vineyard with diverse seeds.*[7] Those commandments whose utility is clear to the multitude are called *mishpaṭim* [*judgments*], and those whose utility is not clear to the multitude are called *ḥuqqim* [*statutes*]. . . .

Chapter 27

The Law as a whole aims at two things: the well-being of the soul and the well-being of the body. As for the well-being of the soul, it consists in the multitude's acquiring correct opinions corresponding to their respective capacity. Therefore some of them [namely, the opinions] are set forth explicitly and some of them are set forth in parables. For it is not within the nature of the common multitude that its capacity should suffice for apprehending that subject matter as it is. As for the well-being of the body, it comes about by the improvement of their ways of living one with another. This is achieved through two things. One of them is the abolition of their wronging one another. This means that every individual among the people is not permitted to act according to his will and up to the limits of his power, but is forced to do what is useful for the whole. The second consists in every individual among the people acquiring moral qualities that are useful for life in society so that the affairs of the city are well ordered. Know that as between these two aims, one is indubitably greater in nobility, namely, the well-being of the soul—I mean the giving of correct opinions— while the second aim—I mean the well-being of the body—is prior in nature and time. The latter aim consists in the governance of the city and the well-being of the states of all its people according to their capacity. This second aim is the more urgent one, and it is the one regarding which every effort has been made to formulate it and all its particulars precisely. For the first aim can only be achieved after achieving this second one. For it has already been demonstrated that man has two perfections: a first perfection, which is the perfection of the body, and an ultimate perfection, which is the perfection of the soul. The first perfection consists in being healthy and in the very best bodily state, and this is only possible through his finding the things necessary for him whenever he seeks them. These are his food and all the other things needed for the governance of his body, such as a shelter, bathing, and so forth. This cannot be achieved in any way by one isolated individual. For an individual can only attain all this through a political association, it being already known that man is political by nature. His ultimate perfection is to become rational in actuality, I mean to have an intellect in actuality: this consists in his knowing everything concerning all the beings that it is within the capacity of man to know in accordance with his ultimate perfection. It is clear that to this ultimate perfection there do not belong either actions or moral qualities and that it consists only of opinions toward which speculation has led and that investigation has rendered compulsory. It is also clear that this noble and ultimate perfection can only be achieved after the first perfection has been achieved. For a man cannot cognize an intelligible even when taught to understand it and all the more cannot become aware of it of his own accord, if he is in pain or is very hungry or is thirsty or is hot or is very cold. But once the first perfection has been achieved it is possible to achieve the ultimate perfection, which is indubitably more noble and is the only cause of permanent preservation.

The true Law then, which as we have already made clear is unique—namely, the Law of *Moses our master*—has come to bring us both perfections, I mean the well-being of the states of people in their relations with one another through the abolition of reciprocal wrongdoing and through the acquisition of a noble and excellent character. In this way the preservation of the inhabitants of the country and their permanent existence in the same order become possible, so that [60b] every one of them achieves his first perfection; and also the soundness of the beliefs and the giving of correct opinions through which ultimate perfection is achieved. The text of the *Torah* speaks of both perfections and informs us that the end of this Law in its entirety is the achievement of these two perfections. For He, may He be exalted, says: *And the Lord commanded us to do all these statutes [ḥuqqim], to fear the Lord our God, for our good always, that He might preserve us alive, as it is at this day.*[1] Here He puts the ultimate perfection first because of its nobility; for, as we have explained, it is the ultimate end. It is referred to in the dictum: *For our good always.* You know already what [the sages], *may their memory be blessed,* have said interpreting His dictum, may He be exalted: *That it may be well with you, and that you may prolong your days.*[2] They said: *That it may be well with you in a world in which everything is well and that you may prolong your days in a world the whole of which is long.*[3] Similarly the intention of His dictum here, *For our good always,* is this same notion: I mean the attainment of *a world in which everything is well* and[*the whole of which is*] *long.* And this is perpetual preservation. On the other hand, His dictum, *That He might preserve us alive, as it is at this day,* refers to the first and corporeal preservation, which lasts for a certain duration and which can only be well ordered through political association, as we have explained.

Chapter 34

Among the things you likewise ought to know is that the Law does not pay attention to the isolated. The Law was not given with a view to things that are rare. For in everything that it wishes to bring about, be it an opinion or a moral habit or a useful work, it is directed only toward the things that occur in the majority of cases and pays no attention to what happens rarely or to the damage occurring to the unique human being because of this way of determination and because of the legal character of the governance. For the Law is a divine thing; and it is your business to reflect on the natural things in which the general utility, which is included in them, nonetheless necessarily produces damages to individuals, as is clear from our discourse and the discourse of others. In view of this consideration also, you will not wonder at the fact that the purpose of the Law is not perfectly achieved in every individual and that, on the contrary, it necessarily follows that there should exist individuals whom this governance of the Law does not make perfect. For not everything that derives necessarily from the natural specific forms is actualized in every individual. Indeed, all things proceed from one deity and one agent and *have been given from one shepherd.*[1] The contrary of this is impossible, and we have already explained that the impossible has a stable nature that never changes.[2] In view of this consideration, it also will not be possible that the laws be dependent on changes in the circumstances of the individuals and of the times, as is the case with regard to medical treatment, which is particularized

for every individual in conformity with his present temperament. On the contrary, governance of the Law ought to be
absolute and general, including everyone, even if it is necessary
only for certain individuals and not necessary for others; for if
it were made to fit individuals, the whole would be corrupted
and *you would make out of it something that varies.*[3] For this reason,
matters that are primarily intended in the Law ought not to be
dependent on time or place; but the decrees ought to be
absolute and general, according to what He, may He be
exalted, says: *As for the congregation, there shall be one statute
[ḥuqqah] for you.*[4] However, only the general interests, those of
the majority, are considered in them, as we have explained.

Chapter 38

The *commandments* comprised in the third class are those that
we have enumerated in *Laws Concerning Character Traits.* The
utility of all of them is clear and evident, for all concern moral
qualities in virtue of which the association among people is in
good condition. This is so manifest that I need not expatiate
upon it. Know that certain *commandments* also contain prescrip-
tions that are intended to lead to the acquisition of a useful
moral quality, even if they prescribe certain actions that are
deemed to be merely *decreed by Scripture* and not to have a
purpose. We will explain them one by one in their proper
places. As for those that we have enumerated in *Laws Concerning Character Traits,* they are all explicitly stated to have as their
purpose the acquisition of the noble moral qualities in question.

Chapter 53

This chapter includes an interpretation of the meaning of three
terms that we have need of interpreting: namely, *ḥesed [loving-
kindness], mishpaṭ [judgment],* and *ṣedaqah [righteousness].*

We have already explained in the Commentary on *Avot*[1] that
the meaning of *ḥesed* is excess in whatever matter excess is
practiced. In most cases, however, it is applied to excess in
beneficence. Now it is known that beneficence includes two
notions, one of them consisting in the exercise of beneficence
toward one who has no right at all to claim this from you, and

the other consisting in the exercise of beneficence toward one who deserves it, but in a greater measure than he deserves. In most cases the prophetic books use the word *hesed* in the sense of practicing beneficence toward one who has no right at all to claim this from you. Therefore every benefit that comes from Him, may He be exalted, is called *hesed*. Thus it says: *I will make mention of the loving-kindnesses [hasdei] of the Lord.*[2] Hence this reality as a whole—I mean His (may He be exalted) bringing it into existence—is *hesed*. Thus it says: *The world is built up in loving-kindness [hesed];*[3] the meaning of which is: *the building up of the world is loving-kindness.* And He, may He be exalted, says in an enumeration of *His attributes: And abundant in loving-kindness.*[4]

The word *sedaqah* is derived from *sedeq*, which means justice; justice being the granting to everyone to whom something is due, that which is due to him, and giving to every being what it deserves. But in the books of the prophets, fulfilling the duties imposed upon you with regard to others is not called *sedaqah* in conformity with the first sense. For if you give a hired man his wages or pay a debt, this is not called *sedaqah*. On the other hand, the fulfilling of duties with regard to others imposed upon you on account of moral virtue, such as remedying the injuries of all those who are injured, is called *sedaqah*. There-fore it says with reference to the returning [131b] of a pledge:[5] *And it shall be sedaqah unto you.*[6] For when you walk in the way of the moral virtues, you do justice unto your rational soul, giving it what is its due. And because every moral virtue is called *sedaqah*, it says: *And he believed in the Lord, and it was accounted to him as sedaqah.*[7] I refer to the virtue of faith. This applies likewise to his dictum, may he be exalted: *And it shall be sedaqah unto us if we take care to observe, and so on.*[8]

As for the word *mishpat*, it means judgment concerning what ought to be done to one who is judged, whether in the way of conferring a benefit or of punishment.

Thus it has been summarized that *hesed* is applied to benefi-cence taken absolutely; *sedaqah*, to every good action performed by you because of a moral virtue with which you perfect your soul; and *mishpat* sometimes has as its consequence punishment and sometimes the conferring of a benefit. When refuting the doctrine of divine attributes, we have already explained that every attribute by which God is described in the books of the prophets is an attribute of action.[9] Accordingly He is described as *ḥasid [one possessing loving-kindness]*[10] because He has brought the whole into being; as *ṣaddiq [righteous]*[11] because of His mercy toward the weak—I refer to the governance of the living being by means of its forces; and as *Judge*[12] because of the occurrence in the world of relative good things and of relative great calamities, necessitated by judgment that is consequent upon wisdom.[13] The *Torah* uses all three terms: *Shall the Judge of all the earth;*[14] *Ṣaddiq [righteous] and upright is He;*[15] *And abundant in ḥesed [loving-kindness].*[16] In interpreting the meaning of these terms, it was our purpose to prepare the way for the chapter that we shall bring after this one.

Chapter 54

The term *wisdom [ḥokhmah]* is applied in Hebrew in four senses. [132a] It is applied to the apprehension of true realities, which have for their end the apprehension of Him, may He be exalted. It says: *But wisdom, where shall it be found? and so on.*[1] It says: *If you seek her as silver, and so on.*[2] This usage is frequent. The term is applied to acquiring arts, whatever the art might be: *And every wise-hearted among you;*[3] *And all the women that were wise-hearted.*[4] It is applied to acquiring moral virtues: *And teach his elders wisdom;*[5] *Is wisdom with aged men?*[6]—for the thing that is acquired through mere old age is a disposition to achieve moral virtues. It is applied to the aptitude for stratagems and ruses: *Come, let us deal wisely with them.*[7] According to this meaning it says: *And fetched from there a wise woman,*[8] meaning thereby that she had an aptitude for stratagems and ruses. In this sense it is said: *They are wise to do evil.*[9] It is possible that the meaning of *wisdom* in Hebrew indicates aptitude for stratagems and the application of thought in such a way that the stratagems and ruses may be used in achieving either rational or moral virtues, or in achieving skill in a practical art, or in working evil and wickedness. It has accordingly become plain that the term *wise* can be applied to one possessing the rational virtues, to one possessing the moral virtues, to everyone skilled in a practical art, and to one possessing ruses in working evil and wickedness. According to this explanation, one who knows the whole of the Law in its true reality is called *wise* in two respects: in respect of the rational virtues comprised in the Law and in respect of the moral virtues included in it. But since the rational matter in the Law is received through tradition and is not demonstrated by the methods of speculation, the knowledge of the Law came to be set up in the books of the prophets and the sayings of the *sages* as one separate species and wisdom,[10] in an unrestricted sense, as another species. It is through this wisdom, in an unrestricted sense, that [132b] the rational matter that we receive from the Law through tradition, is demonstrated. All the texts that you find in the [scriptural] books that extol wisdom and speak of its wonder[11] and of the rarity of those who acquire it—*Now many are wise;*[12] *But wisdom, where shall it be found? and so on;*[13] and many other texts of this kind—treat of that wisdom which teaches us to demonstrate the opinions of the *Torah*. This is also frequent in the sayings of the *sages, may their memory be blessed;* I mean that they set up the knowledge of the *Torah* as one separate species and wisdom as another species. They, *may their memory be blessed,* say of *Moses our master: He was father in wisdom, father in the Torah, father among the prophets.*[14] And with reference to its dictum concerning *Solomon, And he was wiser than all men,*[15] they say: *Not [wiser] than Moses;*[16] for the dictum, *than all men,* means: than his contemporaries. Therefore you will find that it mentions *Heman and Khalkol and Darda, the sons of Mahol,*[17] who were celebrated then as wise men. The *sages, may their memory be blessed,* mention likewise that man is required first to obtain knowledge of the *Torah,* then to obtain wisdom, then to know what is incumbent upon him with regard to the legal science of the Law—I mean the drawing of inferences concerning what one ought to do. And this should be the order observed: The opinions in question should first be known as being received through tradition; then they should be demonstrated; then the actions through which one's way of life may be ennobled, should be precisely defined. This is what they, *may their memory be blessed,* literally say regarding man's being required to give an account with respect to these three matters in this order. They say: *When man comes to judgment, he is first asked: Have you fixed certain seasons for the study of the Torah? Have you ratiocinated concerning wisdom? Have you inferred one thing from another?*[18] It has thus become clear to you that, according to them, the science of the *Torah* is one species and wisdom is a different species, being the verification of the opinions of the *Torah* through correct speculation. After we have made all these preliminary remarks, hear what we shall say:

The ancient [133a] and the modern philosphers have made it clear that the perfections to be found in man consist of four species. The first and the most defective, but with a view to which the people of the earth spend their lives,[19] is the perfection of possessions—that is, of what belongs to the individual in the manner of money, garments, tools, slaves, land, and other things of this kind. A man's being a great king also belongs to this species of perfection. Between this perfection and the individual himself there is no connection whatever; there is only a certain relation, and most of the pleasure taken in the relation is purely imaginary. I refer to one's saying: This is my house; this is my slave; this money is mine; these are my soldiers. For if he considers his own individual self, he will find that all this is outside his essence and that each of these possessions subsists as it is by itself. Therefore when the relation referred to has been abolished, there is no difference between an individual who has been a great king and the most contemptible of men, though nothing may have changed in any of the things that were attributed to him. The philosophers have explained that the endeavor and the efforts directed by man toward this kind of perfection are nothing but an effort with a view to something purely imaginary, to a thing that has no permanence. And even if these possessions should remain with him permanently during the whole of his life, he would by no means thereby achieve perfection with respect to his essence.

The second species has a greater connection than the first with the individual's essence, being the perfection of the bodily constitution and shape—I refer to that individual's temperament being most harmonious, his limbs well proportioned and strong as they ought to be. Neither should this species of perfection be taken as an end, for it is a corporeal perfection and does not belong to man qua man, but qua animal; for man has this in common with the lowest animals. Moreover even if the strength of a human individual reached its greatest [133b] maximum,[20] it would not attain the strength of a strong mule, and still less the strength of a lion or an elephant. The end of this perfection consists, as we have mentioned, in man's transporting a heavy burden or breaking a thick bone and in other things of this kind, from which no great utility for the body may be derived. Utility for the soul is absent from this species of perfection.

The third species is a perfection that to a greater extent than the second species concerns the individual's essence. This is the perfection of the moral virtues. It consists in the individual's moral habits having attained their ultimate excellence.[21] Most of the *commandments* serve no other end than the attainment of this species of perfection. But this species of perfection is likewise a preparation for something else and not an end in itself. For all moral habits are concerned with what occurs between a human individual and someone else. This perfection regarding moral habits is, as it were, the disposition to be useful to people; consequently it is an instrument for someone else. For if you suppose a human individual is alone, acting on no one, you will find that all his moral virtues are in vain and without employment and unneeded, and that they do not perfect the individual in anything; for he only needs them and they again become useful to him in regard to someone else.

The fourth species is the true human perfection; it consists in the acquisition of the rational virtues—I refer to the conception of intelligibles, which teach correct opinions concerning the divine things. This is the final end; this is what gives the individual true perfection, a perfection belonging to him alone; and it gives him permanent perdurance; through it man is man. If you consider each of the three perfections mentioned before, you will find that they pertain to others than you, not to you, even though, according to the generally accepted opinion, they inevitably [134a] pertain both to you and to others. This ultimate perfection, however, pertains to you alone, no one else being associated in it with you in any way: *They shall be only your own, and so on.*[22] Therefore you ought to desire to achieve this thing, which will remain permanently with you, and not weary and trouble yourself for the sake of others, O you who neglect your own soul so that its whiteness has turned into blackness through the corporeal faculties having gained dominion over it

—as is said in the beginning of the poetical parables that have been coined for these notions; it says: *My mother's sons were incensed against me; they made me keeper of the vineyards; but my own vineyard have I not kept.*[23] It says on this very same subject: *Lest you give your splendor to others, and your years to the cruel.*[24]

The prophets, too, have explained to us and interpreted to us the selfsame notions—just as the philosophers have interpreted them—clearly stating to us that neither the perfection of possessions nor the perfection of health nor the perfection of moral habits is a perfection in which one should glory or that one should desire; the perfection in which one should glory and that one should desire is knowledge of Him, may He be exalted, which is the true science. *Jeremiah* says concerning these four perfections: *Thus says the Lord: Let not the wise man glory in his wisdom, neither let the mighty man glory in his might, let not the rich man glory in his riches; but let him that glories glory in this, that he understands and knows Me.*[25] Consider how he mentioned them according to the order given them in the opinion of the multitude. For the greatest perfection in their opinion is that of *the rich man in his riches,* below him *the mighty man in his might,* and below him *the wise man in his wisdom.* [By the expression, "the wise man in his wisdom,"] he means him who possesses the moral virtues; for such an individual is also held in high esteem by the multitude, to whom the discourse in question is addressed. Therefore these perfections are arranged in this order. The *sages, may their memory be blessed,* apprehended from this *verse* the [134b] very notions we have mentioned and have explicitly stated that which I have explained to you in this chapter: namely, that the term *wisdom [hokhmah],* used in an unrestricted sense and regarded as the end, means in every place the apprehension of Him, may He be exalted; that the possession of the treasures acquired, and competed for, by man and thought to be perfection are not a perfection; and that similarly all the actions prescribed by the Law—I refer to the various species of worship and also the moral habits that are useful to all people in their mutual dealings—that all this is not to be compared with this ultimate end and does not equal it, being but preparations made for the sake of this end. Hear verbatim a text of theirs dealing with all these notions; it is a text in *Bereshith Rabbah.* It is said there: *One scriptural dictum says: And all things desirable are not to be compared to her.*[26] *Another scriptural dictum says: And all things you can desire are not to be compared to her.*[27] The expression, *things desirable*, refers to commandments and good actions; while, *things you can desire*, refers to precious stone and pearls. *Neither things desirable nor things you can desire are to be compared to her, but let him that glories glory in this, that he understands and knows Me.*[28] Consider how concise is this saying, how perfect is he who said it, and how he left out nothing of all that we have mentioned and that we have interpreted and led up to at length.

As we have mentioned this *verse* and the wondrous notions contained in it, and as we have mentioned the saying of the *sages, may their memory be blessed,* about it, we will complete the exposition of what it includes. For when explaining in this *verse* the noblest ends, he does not limit them only to the apprehension of Him, may He be exalted. For if this were his purpose, he would have said: *But let him that glories glory in this, that he understands and knows Me,* and have stopped there; or he would have said: *that he understands and knows Me that I am One;* or he would have said: *that I have no figure,* or that [135a] *there is none like Me,* or something similar. But he says that one should glory in the apprehension of Myself and in the knowledge of My attributes, by which he means His actions, as we have made clear[29] with reference to its dictum: *Show me now Your ways, and so on.*[30] In this *verse*[31] he makes it clear to us that those actions that ought to be known and imitated are *loving-kindness [ḥesed], judgment [mishpaṭ]* and *righteousness [ṣedaqah].* He adds another corroborative notion through saying, *in the earth*[32]—this being a pivot of the Law. For matters are not as the overbold opine who think that His providence, may He be exalted, terminates at the sphere of the moon and that the earth and that which is in it are neglected: *The Lord has forsaken the earth.*[33] Rather is it as has been made clear to us by the master of those who know: *That the earth is the Lord's.*[34] He means to say that His providence also extends over the earth in the way that corresponds to what the latter is, just as His providence extends over the heavens[35] in the way that corresponds to what they are. This is what he says: *That I am the Lord who exercises loving-kindness, judgment, and righteousness, in the earth.*[36] Then he completes the notion by saying: *For in these things I delight, says the Lord.*[37] He means that it is My purpose that there should come from you *loving-kindness, righteousness, and judgment in the earth* in the way we have explained with regard to the *thirteen attributes:*[38] namely, that the purpose should be assimilation to them and that this should be our way of life. Thus the end that he sets forth in this *verse* may be stated as follows: It is clear that the perfection of man that may truly be gloried in is the one acquired by him who has achieved, in a measure corresponding to his capacity, apprehension of Him, may He be exalted, and who knows His providence extending over His creatures as manifested in the act of bringing them into being and in their governance as it is. The way of life of such an individual, after he has achieved this apprehension, will always have in view *loving-kindness, righteousness,* and *judgment,* through assimilation to His actions, may He be exalted, just as we have explained several times in this treatise.

NOTES

PART I

Chapter 2

1. Gen. 3:5
2. *ma'ānī*. The term has many meanings and often, as in this passage, cannot be satisfactorily translated.
3. The Arabic verb sometimes designates a particular kind of transmigration.
4. The word may also refer to the scriptural story, but the translation given in the text is somewhat more probable.
5. Gen. 2:16.
6. Or: fine (*al-ḥasan*).
7. The expression, "generally accepted opinions," renders the Arabic term *al-mashhūrāt*, which is used as a translation of the Greek *endoxa*.
8. In Hebrew.
9. Ps. 8:6.
10. Gen. 3:6.
11. Gen. 3:5.
12. Gen. 3:7.
13. Used in the verse.
14. Gen. 21:19.
15. Isa. 35:5.
16. Isa. 42:20.
17. Ezek. 12:2.
18. Job 14:20.
19. The Arabic word derives from a root from which the usual word for "face" is likewise derived.
20. The Hebrew word for "face."
21. Gen. 3:18–19.
22. Gen. 3:23.
23. Gen. 3:18.
24. Or: man.
25. Ps. 49:13.

PART II

Chapter 33

1. Deut. 5:5.
2. Exod. 19:19.

3. *Mekhilta,* commentary on Exod. 20:1.
4. Exod. 19:19.
5. Deut. 5:20.
6. Deut. 4:12.
7. In the text: *Midrashot.*
8. *B.T.,* Makkot, 24a; *Midrash on the Song of Songs,* 1:2.
9. I.e., the First Commandment.
10. I.e., the Second Commandment.
11. The Hebrew word *geburah,* here translated "force," sometimes designates the deity.
12. Literally: roots.
13. Deut. 4:35.
14. See *infra, Logic,* VIII.

Chapter 40

1. I.e., the human species.
2. Or: temperaments.
3. Law.
4. I.e., the prophet and the one who lays down the nomos.
5. Cf. I Kings 22:11 and 24.
6. Cf. Jer. 28:1 ff.
7. Or: governances. The text has the plural.
8. I.e., composed of man-made laws.
9. *madīnah,* i.e., *polis.*
10. The expression used is *sharī'ah nāmūsiyyah*; literally: nomic Law. *nāmūsiyyah* derives from *nāmūs,* which is the Arabic form of the Greek word *nomos.* It signifies in the context a law promulgated by a legislator who was not a prophet.
11. Cf. *Nicomachean Ethics* iii.10, 1118b2ff. The passage referring to the sense of touch reads as follows in Rackham's translation: "Hence the sense to which profligacy is related is the most universal of the senses; and there appears to be good ground for the disrepute in which it is held, because it belongs to us not as human beings but as animals."
12. Jer. 29:22–23.

PART III

Chapter 26

1. Deut. 4:8.
2. Ps. 19:10.
3. This Hebrew term is sometimes interpreted as designating those religious laws that have no (or no obvious) explanation in terms of human reason. Cf. *C.M.,* Eight Chapters, VI.

4. Cf. Deut. 22:11; Exod. 23:19; Lev. 16:10 and 21.
5. *B.T.*, Yoma, 67b.
6. Literally: *foreskin*. Cf. Lev. 19:23.
7. Cf. Deut. 22:9.

Chapter 27

1. Deut. 6:24.
2. Deut. 22:7.
3. *B.T.*, Qiddushin, 39b; Hullin, 142a.

Chapter 34

1. Eccles. 12:11.
2. *Guide*, III 15.
3. Cf., e.g., *B.T.*, Shabbat, 35b; Hullin, 9a.
4. Num. 15:15.

Chapter 53

1. *C.M.*, Avot, V 6, and II 10.
2. Isa. 63:7.
3. Ps. 89:3. In the English Bible: *For ever is mercy built.*
4. Exod. 34:6.
5. To the poor.
6. Deut. 24:13.
7. Gen. 15:6.
8. Deut. 6:25.
9. *Guide*, I 52–54.
10. A word deriving from the same verbal root as *hesed.*
11. A word deriving from the same verbal root as *sedaqah.*
12. *Shophet,* a word deriving from the same verbal root as *mishpat.*
13. The Arabic word for "judgment" (*hukm*) derives from the same verbal root as the Arabic word for "wisdom" (*hikmah*).
14. Gen. 18:25.
15. Deut. 32:4.
16. Exod. 34:6.

Chapter 54

1. Job 28:12.
2. Prov. 2:4.
3. Exod. 35:10.
4. Exod. 35:25.
5. Ps. 105:22.

6. Job 12:12.
7. Exod. 1:10.
8. II Sam. 14:2.
9. Jer. 4:22.
10. It is not quite clear whether Maimonides uses here the Hebrew word *hokhmah* or the Arabic word *hikmah*, each of which is written in the same way in Judeo-Arabic. The Arabic word also connotes "philosophy." The Hebrew word may also have this connotation, and if Maimonides used it here, he undoubtedly had this connotation in mind.
11. Or: its strangeness.
12. Job 32:9.
13. Job 28:12.
14. *B.T.*, Megillah, 13a.
15. I Kings 5:11.
16. *B.T.*, Rosh Hashanah, 21b.
17. I Kings 5:11.
18. *B.T.*, Shabbat, 31a.
19. Or: mutually destroy each other.
20. Literally: finality and end.
21. The Arabic word *fadīlah*, translated "excellence," is the singular of the word translated in the preceding sentence as "virtues."
22. Prov. 5:17.
23. Song of Songs 1:6.
24. Prov. 5:9.
25. Jer. 9:22–23.
26. Prov. 8:11.
27. Prov. 3:15.
28. *Genesis Rabbah,* XXXV *in fine.*
29. Cf. *Guide,* I 54.
30. Exod. 33:13.
31. Jer. 9:23 is referred to.
32. Jer. 9:23.
33. Ezek. 9:9.
34. Exod. 9:29.
35. In the singular in Arabic.
36. Jer. 9:23.
37. Jer. 9:23.
38. Cf. *Guide,* I 54.

VI

TREATISE ON THE ART OF LOGIC

The *Logic* is a short work written in response to a request by a
jurist for a concise account of the terms used in logic. It appears
to be based to a considerable extent upon the logical works of
al-Fārābī, for whom Maimonides had a high regard.

Logic is relevant to ethics in a number of respects. It contains
a discussion of modalities, including those which pertain to
ethics (III). It specifies the different kinds of premises used in
argumentation, including practical reasoning (VIII). And,
since logic is an instrument used in all of the sciences, Maimonides includes a brief account of the areas to which it is applied.
Logic, then, also contains a classification of the sciences, including the practical sciences (XIV).

There are fourteen chapters in the *Logic*. The selections
below include part of Chapter Three and all of Chapters Eight
and Fourteen.

TREATISE ON THE ART OF LOGIC

CHAPTER THREE

. . . An utterance indicating the way the predicate of a proposition is related to the subject may be joined to the predicate, as when we say: "possible," "impossible," "probable," "by necessity," "obligatory," "necessary," "base," "noble," "ought," "must," and the like. These utterances and their like may occur in a bipartite or tripartite proposition.[1] We call these utterances and their like modalities. For instance, when we say, "It is possible for man to write," "possible" is a modality. Similarly when we say, "Every man is necessarily an animal," "necessarily" is a modality. Again, when we say "Zayd must stand," "It is base for Zayd to insult [others]," "Zayd ought to know," and "It is probable that Zayd will act like that," we call all of these modalities. We call the verb a word, and verbs we call words. . . .

CHAPTER EIGHT

There are four kinds of propositions which are known and require no proof of their validity: (1) sense perceptions, such as our knowing that this is black, this is sweet, and this is hot; (2) first intelligibles, such as our knowing that the whole is greater than the part, that two is an even number, and that things equal to the same thing are all equal to each other; (3) generally accepted opinions, such as our knowing that uncovering the genitals is base and that compensating a benefactor generously is noble; and (4) traditions, which include everything received from a sanctioned individual or sanctioned assembly. We seek proof only concerning the general trustworthiness of the individual from whom something is received, not concerning every statement he utters. Rather he is met with complete acceptance, if his general trustworthiness has been validated by everything said about him.

For members of the human species with healthy senses and dispositions,[1] there is no controversy about sense perceptions and intelligibles. Nor is there any contention[2] concerning the certainty to which they attest. However, there is controversy and contention[2] about generally accepted opinions. Indeed, there are propositions which are generally accepted within one nation, but not within another nation. Moreover, whenever something is generally accepted within many nations, it carries more powerful conviction. The same holds with regard to traditions: that which is received by one people might not be received by another.

Whenever someone perceives something by means of a healthy sense [organ], he is undoubtedly certain of it. Likewise, all of the first and second intelligibles are certain. (By second intelligibles I mean, for example, geometrical forms and astronomical calculations. All of these are certainly intelligibles, because they are explained by premises which ultimately depend on first intelligibles.) So too, whatever experience confirms is certain, like the purgative effect of scammony on the stomach, the constipating effect of gallnut, and similar things. Whenever knowledge is attained by one of these three means,[3] the logicians call the resulting proposition apodeictic.[4]

After this introduction, you should know that we call every syllogism both of whose premises are apodeictic a demonstrative syllogism. The use of these syllogisms and knowledge of their conditions we call the art of demonstration. When one or both of the premises of a syllogism is based on what is generally accepted, we call it a dialectical syllogism. The art of dialectic is the use of these syllogisms and knowledge of their conditions. When one or both of the premises of a syllogism is based on tradition,[5] we call it a rhetorical syllogism. The art of rhetoric is the use of these syllogisms and knowledge of the ways they are used. There is another kind of syllogism, in which deception and distortion are used. Syllogisms are designated as sophistical when their premises—one or both of them—are such as to deceive, lead into error, or distort. The use of these syllogisms and knowledge of the ways by which one deceives and distorts may be called the art of sophistry. Simply by simile and comparison things may be presented in a favorable light or made repugnant. Every syllogism with a premise set down as a simile or comparison we call a poetic syllogism. The art which uses these syllogisms and teaches how to construct the comparison and the analogy which it uses is called the art of poetics.

Know that the demonstrative syllogisms have conditions

which need not be mentioned in this discussion. However, analogy is not used at all in the demonstrative syllogisms, and induction is used only under certain conditions. It is the art of dialectic which uses induction without restriction, and the art of rhetoric uses an analogical syllogism. Likewise, one premise of the rhetorical syllogism is disclosed and the other hidden for certain reasons. This is what we call an enthymeme.[6]

The total number of terms whose meanings I have explained in this chapter is seventeen. They are: sense perceptions, first intelligibles, second intelligibles, generally accepted opinions, traditions, apodeictic[7] proposition, demonstrative syllogism, art of demonstration, dialectical syllogism, art of dialectic, rhetorical syllogism, art of rhetoric, sophistical syllogism, art of sophistry, poetic syllogism, art of poetics, enthymeme.[8]

CHAPTER FOURTEEN

According to the technical usage of the ancient learned men of past communities,[1] "logic"[2] is an equivocal[3] term having three meanings. The first is the power peculiar[4] to man by which he intellectually apprehends the intelligibles, masters[5] the arts, and distinguishes between the base and the noble. They call this meaning the rational[6] power. The second meaning is the intelligible itself which man has intellectually apprehended. They call this[7] meaning "internal reason."[8] The third meaning is the expression in language of the notions impressed upon the soul. They call this meaning "external reason."[9]

Aristotle set down this art and perfected its parts in eight books. It gives the rational power rules concerning the intelligibles, i.e., internal reason, so that it will be guarded from error and shown the way to what is correct. In this way it will acquire certainty concerning everything which[10] it is in man's power to acquire certainty about. This art also gives rules which are common to all languages, by which external reason is shown the way to what is correct and is guarded from error. In this way what is expressed by the tongue conforms to what is in the mind and is identical with it; the expression neither surpasses, nor is inadequate to, the notion which is in the soul. Because of the concepts which this art provides, they [the ancients] called it the art of logic. They said that the rank of the art of logic with respect to the intellect is the same as that of the art of grammar with respect to language.

According to the ancients, the term "art" is equivocal. They apply it to every speculative science as well as to the practices employed in crafts. Thus they call each of the philosophic sciences a speculative art; carpentry, rope-making, sewing, and the like, they call practical arts.

This term "philosophy" is also equivocal. Sometimes they use it to denote the art of demonstration and sometimes they use it to denote the sciences. According to them, this term applies to two sciences in particular. One of the two sciences, they call practical philosophy. They also call it human philosophy as well as political science. Theoretical philosophy is divided into three parts: the first is the science of mathematics, the second is natural science, and the third is divine science.

The science of mathematics does not investigate bodies as such, but rather ideas[11] abstracted from their matter—even if those ideas[11] are found only in matter. The parts of this science, which are its roots, are four. They are: the science of arithmetic; the science of geometry; the science of the stars, by which I mean astronomy; and the science of the composition of melodies, which is music. They call all of these parts the mathematical sciences.

Natural science investigates the bodies existing by nature, not by the will of man—such as the species of minerals, plants, and animals. Natural science investigates all of these bodies; whatever is found in them, I mean, all of their accidents, properties, and causes;[12] and everything in which these bodies are necessarily found—such as time, place, and motion.

Divine science is divided into two parts. One [part] is the investigation of every being which is neither a body nor a power in a body. It is the discourse about what pertains to the deity, may His name be magnified. According to the opinion [of the ancients] it is also a discourse about the angels, for they do not believe the angels to be corporeal. Rather, they call them separate intellects, meaning thereby that the angels are separate from matter. The second part of divine science investigates the very remote causes for everything which all the other sciences encompass. They call this part both divine science and metaphysics.[13] These, in sum, are the sciences of the first things.

According to the ancients, the art of logic is not one of the sciences. Rather, it is a tool for the sciences. They said that instruction or study proceeds in an orderly manner only through the art of logic. It is therefore a tool for everything, and the tool for something is not part of the thing.

Political science is divided into four parts. The first is the individual's governance of himself; the second is the governance of the household; the third is the governance of the city; and the fourth is the governance of the large nation or of the nations.

Man's governance of himself consists in making his soul acquire the virtuous moral habits and cease to have the vicious moral habits, if any have been formed. The moral habits are the settled states which form in the soul in such a way that they become fixed dispositions from which actions stem. The philosophers speak of moral habits in terms of virtue and vice. They call the noble moral habits, moral virtues, and they call the base moral habits, moral vices. The actions stemming from the virtuous moral habits they call good, and the actions stemming from the vicious moral habits they call bad. Likewise, they speak of reason—that is, conceiving the intelligibles—in terms of virtue and vice. Hence they speak of rational virtues and rational vices. The philosophers have many books about the moral habits. Every governance by which one man governs another, they call a regime.

The governance of the household consists in knowing how some [members of the household] help others and what they must be restricted to, so that their condition will be well ordered as far as the requirements of that time and place permit.

The governance of the city is a science which provides its inhabitants with the knowledge of true happiness along with the way of striving to attain it; the knowledge of true misery along with the way of striving to keep it away; and the way of training their moral habits to reject the presumed kinds of happiness so that they do not take delight in them or covet them. It explains the presumed kinds of misery to them so that they do not suffer from them or dread them. Similarly, it prescribes laws of justice for them by which they can order their communities. The learned men of past communities,[14] each according to his perfection, used to fashion regimes[15] and laws by which their kings would govern the subjects. They called them nomoi,[16] and the nations used to be governed by those nomoi. The philosophers have many books about all of these things which have already been translated into Arabic. Those that have not been translated are perhaps even more numerous. In these times all that—I mean, the regimes and the nomoi—has been dispensed with, and people are governed by divine commands.

All of the terms whose meanings I have explained in this chapter total twenty-five. They are: rational power, internal reason, external reason, art of logic, speculative arts, practical arts, philosophy, theoretical philosophy, practical philosophy, human philosophy, political science, mathematics, mathematical sciences, natural science, divine science, metaphysics, moral habits, moral virtues, moral vices, rational virtues, rational vices, good,[17] bad,[17] regime, nomoi. . . .

NOTES

CHAPTER THREE

1. Bipartite propositions consist of a subject and a verbal predicate, or of a subject, verbal predicate, and its object. Examples of such propositions given by Maimonides are: "Zayd stood," "Zayd killed Abū Bakr," "Zayd did not stand," and "Zayd did not kill Abū Bakr." Propositions of this sort are called bipartite because no additional word is needed to connect the predicate with the subject. However, when the predicate is a gerund, an additional word is needed to connect the predicate with the subject, and the proposition is therefore called tripartite. Examples of such propositions given by Maimonides are: "Zayd is standing now," "Zayd was standing," and "Zayd will be standing."

CHAPTER EIGHT

1. The Arabic word is *fiṭar*; in *C.M.*, Eight Chapters, VIII, it is translated as "inborn dispositions."
2. Reading *tafāḍul*; see Efros, p. 157, note 1.
3. Reading *al-thalāth al-ṭuruq* instead of *al-ṭuruq* (Efros), and instead of *al-thulth ṭuruq* (Türker).
4. This is the same word which was previously translated as "certain."
5. Reading *maqbūlah* (Türker), instead of *maqbīlah* (Efros).
6. Reading *al-ḍamā'ir*; see Efros, p. 157, note 3. The Arabic word is in the plural.
7. Cf. note four.
8. Cf. note six.

CHAPTER FOURTEEN

1. *Milal* has the primary meaning of "religious communities," but Maimonides apparently meant to use it here in the secondary sense of "national communities."
2. The Arabic word for logic (*manṭiq*) is derived from a verb which can either mean to reason or to speak.
3. In Chapter Thirteen of the *Treatise on the Art of Logic*, Maimonides explained that an equivocal noun has several meanings. An example in English would be "ball," which refers to a spherical object or to a particular kind of festive party.

4. Reading *yukhtaṣṣ,* instead of *tukhtaṣṣ* (Efros).
5. Reading *yaḥūz* instead of Efros' suggested emendation to *yaghūd* (p. 159, note 16) and instead of Türker's *yajūr.* See D. M. Dunlop, "al-Fārābī's Introductory *Risālah* on Logic," in *Islamic Quarterly,* III (1957), p. 228, line 2 and p. 233, lines 2–3. The language and the arguments are sufficiently similar to suppose that Maimonides used the same verb as al-Fārābī. This emendation requires simply changing the diacritical points, not substituting a different letter.
6. Or: speaking (*nāṭiq*).
7. Reading *hādhā* (Türker), instead of *hādhīhī* (Efros).
8. Or: "inner speech (*al-nuṭq al-dākhil*)."
9. Or: "external speech (*al-nuṭq al-khārij*)."
10. Reading *bi kullimā* with Ibn Tibbon, Aḥitub, and Vivas (*bekhol mah*).
11. *ma'ānī.* The term has many meanings and is very difficult to render in English. In this section, it has also been translated as meaning, notion, and concept.
12. Reading *wa asbābihā* with Ibn Tibbon and Vivas (*wesibotam*) and Aḥitub (*wesiboteihem*); Efros omits *wa.*
13. Reading *wa mā ba'd al- tabī'ah* with Ibn Tibbon, Aḥitub, and Vivas (*umah she-'aher ha-ṭeva'*). If the omission of *wa* ("and") in the Efros edition were accepted, the sentence would have to be translated: "They also call this divine metaphysical science." Maimonides never refers to metaphysics in that way.
14. See note one.
15. Or: ways of governing.
16. The Arabic *nawāmīs* is almost a direct transliteration from the Greek *nomoi,* meaning laws or conventions.
17. The text has the plural.

VII

THE DAYS OF THE MESSIAH

The following selections pertaining to the messianic era are drawn from three different sources. The first selection, from the *Commentary on the Mishnah,* is excerpted from the lengthy commentary by Maimonides on the rabbinic statement: "All Israel has a portion (*ḥeleq*) in the world-to-come" (*Mishnah,* Sanhedrin, X 1). The entire commentary on this passage has come to be known as *Pereq Ḥeleq (Chapter on "Portion").* His discussion of the world-to-come impels him to distinguish the next world, or the immortality of the soul, from the days of the messiah, which will take place in this world. *Pereq Ḥeleq* also contains his formulation of the thirteen foundations of the Law. Only the twelfth foundation, dealing with the days of the messiah, is included here.

Following the excerpts from *Pereq Ḥeleq* are selections from the two parts of the Code in which the messianic era is described: *Laws Concerning Repentance* and *Laws of Kings and Their Wars.* In the former section, the subject of repentance leads to a discussion of the benefits derived from fulfilling the Law—the greatest benefit is to merit the world-to-come—and the dire consequences of sin. Because of the oppression that prevented complete devotion to the Law, the prophets and sages yearned for the messianic era, which is discussed briefly in Chapter Nine of *Laws Concerning Repentance.* The last two chapters of *Laws of Kings and Their Wars* are also translated here, including the passage referring to Jesus and Muhammad (XI 4), which had been expunged from the traditional versions. Earlier in this section, Maimonides sets forth the laws for establishing and governing the future monarchy, and then, at the very end of the Code, the coming of the messianic king is described.

Maimonides touches briefly on the messianic era in the *Guide* within the broader context of his discussion of how evil could exist, given the goodness of God. The short chapter from the *Guide* included below describes how evil will eventually be overcome at the end of days.

COMMENTARY ON THE MISHNAH
PEREQ HELEQ

The days of the messiah will occur when rule returns to *Israel* and they[1] return to Palestine.[2] This king who arises [in the future] will have the seat of his rule in *Zion*. His fame will be great, reaching to the ends of the earth; it will be even greater than that of King *Solomon*. Because of his consummate justice, 'the religious communities will make peace with him and the nations will obey him. Miracles will appear through him.[3] God Himself will cut off and destroy anyone who rises up against him.

All the verses of the *Bible* testify to his happiness and to our happiness that will come about through him. Nothing at all in existence will change from the way it is now, except that *Israel* will have a kingdom. The text of the *sages* is as follows: *There is no difference between this world and the days of the messiah, except for [the elimination of] subjugation to the [wicked] kingdoms.*[4] In his days, the powerful and the weak will [still] be distinguished from one another.[5] However, in those days, a livelihood will come much easier to people, so that a man will labor less and reap great benefit. This is the meaning of their saying: *In the future, the land of Israel will yield fine bread and woolen garments.*[6] For when someone finds something already prepared and in abundance, people say that so-and-so found baked bread and cooked food. Your proof for this is the verse, *And foreigners shall be your plowmen and vinedressers,*[7] which proves that there will then be cultivated and harvested land. Therefore, this *sage*[8] who said the above became angry at his student for not understanding the meaning and for taking the statement literally. Hence, he answered him according to the level of his perception, but this is not the [correct] answer. The proof that he did not give him the true explanation is that the basis for his reply was the verse: *Do not answer the fool according to his folly.*[9]

The great benefit of that time is that we shall be redeemed from *the subjugation to the wicked kingdom,* which hinders us from acquiring all the virtues. Knowledge will increase, as he [Isaiah] said: *For the earth shall be full of the knowledge of the Lord.*[10] Civil strife and wars will cease, as he [Micah] said: *And nation shall not lift up sword against nation.*[11] Whoever is alive in those days will attain much perfection and be elevated *to the life of the world-to-come.* The *messiah* will die, his son will succeed him, and then his grandson. God has explained that he [the messiah] will die. He said: *He shall not fail nor be crushed until he establishes justice in the earth, etc.*[12] His kingdom will last an extremely long time. The duration of life will also increase, because with the removal of grief and hardship the duration of life increases. It would not be surprising if his dominion lasted for thousands of years. For the wise men have said that if the virtuous community comes into existence, it is unlikely that it will disintegrate.

Do not wish for the days of the *messiah* so that crops and wealth will increase or so that we ride fine steeds and drink [wine] accompanied by music, as people with confused intellects think. The prophets longed for them [the days of the messiah] and the virtuous men ardently desired them because there will then be a virtuous community, a fine way of life, knowledge, and a king who is just, great in knowledge, and close to His Creator—as He said to him: *You are My son.*[13] The entire Law of *Moses* will be obeyed, without weariness, worry, or oppression. As He promised:[14] *A man shall not teach his neighbor, etc. For they shall all know Me, from the least of them to the greatest;*[15] *And I will place My Law in their heart;*[16] *And I will remove the heart of stone from your flesh.*[17] Many such passages express the same intentions. The above conditions give powerful [assistance] for attaining *the life of the world-to-come;* the purpose is *the world-to-come,* which one must strive to attain.

Therefore this man,[18] who was certain of the truth, looked to the ultimate goal and ignored everything else. So he said: *All Israel has a portion in the world-to-come.*[19] Although that is the purpose, someone who wishes to *serve out of love* should not serve in order to attain *the world-to-come,* as we have explained in what preceded.[20] Rather, he should serve in the way I shall describe.

If he believes that knowledge came to the prophets from God who thereby taught them that the virtues and vices are thus and so, it is incumbent upon him, insofar as he is an equitable man, to pursue the virtues and avoid the vices. If he does so, the meaning of man will be perfected in him and he will be distinguished from the beasts. When a man achieves perfection, he is in the class of the man who is not hampered by any obstacle that would prevent his soul from remaining permanently with its knowledge. This is *the world-to-come,* as we have explained. And this is the meaning of his [the psalmist's] saying: *Do not be like a horse or a mule, without understanding, [which must be curbed with bit and bridle].*[21] He means that what keeps them from running free is something external, like a bit or a bridle. Man is not like that, but what keeps him from [a comparable freedom] is his soul, I mean, his human form. If it is perfect, it keeps him away from what perfection guards against, namely, vices, and it spurs him on to that which perfects him, which are the virtues. This is what I have arrived at from all of their[22] statements about this lofty, great, and momentous idea.

*   *   *

[The following is among the thirteen foundations of the Law.]

The twelfth foundation, *the days of the messiah,* [entails] faith in and affirmation of his coming, not finding him slow in coming—*If he tarries, wait for him*[23]—and not setting a fixed time for him. Do not interpret the texts in order to infer the time of his coming. The *sages* say: *May the knowledge of those who calculate the end*[24] *expire.*[25] Belief in him includes glorifying and loving [him] and praying for him, in accordance with what is stated about him by every prophet from *Moses* to *Malachi.* Whoever has doubts about him or makes light of any matter connected with him, imputes falsehood to the *Torah,* which made unambiguous promises about him in the *Section on Balaam*[26] and in *You stand.*[27] Included in this foundation is [the belief] that the king of *Israel* can be only from [the house of] *David,* specifically from the line of *Solomon.* Anyone who contradicts what concerns this lineage expresses heresy toward God and the texts of His prophets.

MISHNEH TORAH

LAWS CONCERNING REPENTANCE

Chapter Nine

1. It has become known that the life of the world-to-come is the reward for performing the commandments and is the good that we merit if we have kept the way of the Lord referred to in the Torah. As it is said: "So that it shall be good for you and you shall prolong your days."[1] And being cut off is the revenge that is exacted from the wicked who have forsaken the paths of justice referred to in the Torah. As it is said: "That soul shall be completely cut off; his iniquity shall be upon him."[2] What, then, is meant by verses found throughout the entire Torah, saying: "If you obey, there will come to you . . . and if you do not obey, there will befall you. . . ." And [what is meant by the reference to] all those things that occur in *this*[3] world, such as satiety and hunger, war and peace, rule and submission, the settlement of the land [of Israel] and Exile, prosperity and failure, and everything else mentioned in the covenant?

2. It is true that all these things have taken place and will take place. When we perform all the commandments of the Torah, all that is good[4] in this world will come to us. When we transgress them, the prescribed evils will befall us. Nevertheless, those good things are not the final reward given for performing the commandments, nor are those evils the final revenge exacted for transgressing all the commandments. The explanation of these matters is as follows.

3. The Holy One, blessed be He, gave us the Torah; this is the tree of life. Everyone who does everything prescribed therein and knows it completely and correctly,[5] merits the life of the world-to-come. His merit depends upon how great his actions and his wisdom are. He [God] promised us in the Torah that if we follow it with joy and a glad soul[6] and we continually meditate on its wisdom, He will remove from us everything preventing us from following it—such as sickness, war, hunger, and so forth—and He will cause an overflow toward us of all the good things that strengthen us in following the entire Torah—such as satiety, peace, and an abundance of silver and gold.

4. [The purpose is] that we not be occupied all our days with things needed by the body, but that we have the leisure to learn wisdom and to perform the commandments[7] so that we merit the life of the world-to-come. Thus, after He promised the benefits of this world, it says in the Torah: "And there shall be justice for us, etc."[8]

5. So too, He informed us in the Torah that if we intentionally forsake the Torah and become occupied with the vanities of the time—as it is said, "And Jeshuran grew fat and rebelled, etc."[9]—the Judge of the truth will remove from the sinners[10] all the good things of the world that strengthen their hands for rebellion, and will bring upon them all the evils that prevent them from possessing the world-to-come, so that they perish in their wickedness. That is written in the Torah: "And you shall serve your enemies, whom the Lord shall send against you, etc., because you did not serve the Lord your God with joy and a glad heart, due to the abundance of everything."[11]

6. The explanation of all those blessings and curses is similar. That is to say, if you serve the Lord in joy and follow His way, He causes an overflow of those blessings toward you and keeps away the curses, so that you have the leisure to become wise in the Torah and to be occupied with it, in order that you merit the life of the world-to-come. He will benefit you with a world that is totally good and lengthen your days in a world whose length does not end. You will merit both worlds: a good life in this world, which brings about the life of the world-to-come. For if one does not acquire wisdom and good deeds here, he has nothing with which to merit [the world-to-come]. As it is said: "For there is neither deed nor thought nor knowledge nor wisdom in Sheol, etc."[12]

7. If you forsake the Lord and go astray through eating, drinking, fornication, and the like, He will bring upon you all those curses and remove all the blessings, so that you reach the point where your days are consumed in terror and dread. Your heart will not be free[13] nor your body perfect to perform the commandments, so that you will lose the life of the world-to-come. You will have lost both worlds, for when a man is burdened in this world with sickness, war, and famine, he occupies himself with neither wisdom nor commandment, through which one merits the life of the world-to-come.

8. Because of this all Israel, its prophets as well as its wise

men, longed for the days of the messianic king, so that they would be liberated from the wicked kingdom that does not allow Israel to be occupied with the Torah and with the commandments in the proper way, and so that they would find repose and increase [their] wisdom in order to merit the life of the world-to-come.

9. For at that time knowledge, wisdom, and truth will increase. As it is said: "For the earth shall be full of knowledge of the Lord";[14] "And a man shall no longer teach his brother or his neighbor, etc.";[15] "And I will remove the heart of stone from your flesh."[16] [All this will take place] because the king who will arise from the seed of David will possess more wisdom than Solomon and be a great prophet, closer than Moses our master.[17] Therefore he will teach all the people and show them the way of the Lord, and all the nations will come to hear him. As it is said: "And it shall come to pass at the end of days that the mountain of the Lord's house shall be established as the top of the mountains, etc."[18]

10. The complete, final reward and the ultimate good that does not cease nor diminish is the life of the world-to-come. However, the days of the messiah are in this world. The world will go along in accordance with its custom, except that rule will return to Israel. The wise men of old[19] have already said: "There is no difference between this world and the days of the messiah, except for [the elimination of] subjugation to the [wicked] kingdoms."[20]

*   *   *

LAWS OF KINGS AND THEIR WARS

Chapter Eleven

1. The messianic king will arise in the future and restore the kingdom of David as it was of old in the first dominion. He will rebuild the sanctuary, gather the dispersed of Israel, and restore all the laws[1] in his days as they were before. They [the people] will bring sacrifices and observe the Sabbatical and Jubilee years in accordance with everything that has been commanded in the Torah. Anyone who does not believe in him or does not await his coming repudiates not only the other prophets, but Moses our master and the Torah as well. The

Torah did indeed give testimony about him. As it is said: "And
the Lord your God will turn your captivity and have mercy
upon you and return and gather you, etc. If your dispersion
will reach the extremity of the heavens, etc. And the Lord will
bring you [to the land which your fathers possessed]."[2] These
are the explicit words of the Torah and they encompass all the
words that were spoken by all the prophets.

It is even spoken about in the section [of the Torah] dealing
with Balaam, who prophesied about both messiahs: the first
messiah, David, who saved Israel from the hand of their
enemies, and the final messiah, who will arise from his descendants and save Israel from the hand of the sons of Esau.[3] He
[Balaam] says there: "I see him, but not now"[4]—that is David;
"I behold him, but not near"—that is the messianic king. "A star
will come forth out of Jacob"—that is David; "A scepter will rise
out of Israel"—that is the messianic king. "He will crush the
forehead of Moab"—that is David, for thus it says: "And he
smote Moab and measured them with a line."[5] [Balaam said:]
"He will break down all the sons of Seth"[6]—that is the messianic
king. As it is said about him: "And his dominion will be from
sea to sea."[7] [Balaam said:] "And Edom will be a possession"[8]—
that is David. As it is said: "And the Edomites became slaves of
David, etc."[9] [Balaam said:] "And [Seir] will be a possession,
etc."[10]—that is the messianic king. As it is said: "And saviors will
go up to Mount Zion, etc."[11]

2. Even concerning the cities of refuge, he [Moses] says: "If
the Lord your God extends your border . . . and you shall add
three more cities for yourself, etc."[12] This never took place and
the Holy One, blessed be He, does not give a commandment
for nought. As for the words of the prophets, the matter needs
no proof, for all [their] books are full of this matter.

3. Do not suppose that the messianic king needs to give signs,
perform miracles, and make new things happen in the world,
or resurrect the dead and do similar things. It is not so. Rabbi
Akiba, a great wise man among the wise men of the *Mishnah*,
was an armorbearer of King ben Koziba, and said that the latter
was the messianic king.[13] He [Akiba] and all the wise men of his
generation imagined him to be the messianic king, until he [ben
Koziba] was slain because of the sins.[14] When he was slain, it
became clear to them that he was not [the messianic king]. Now,

the wise men did not ask him for a sign or a miracle. The root of these matters is as follows: this Torah, with its statutes and judgments, will last forever and ever. It is not permitted to add to them or delete any of them.

4. If a king arises from the house of David who meditates on the Torah and performs the commandments like his forefather, David, in accordance with the Written and the Oral Law; who compels all Israel to follow it and to repair its breaches; and who fights the wars of the Lord—he is considered to be the messiah. If he succeeds in what he does and he rebuilds the sanctuary on its site and gathers the dispersed of Israel, he is certainly the messiah. He will prepare the whole world to serve the Lord together. As it is said: "For then I will change the speech of the peoples to a pure speech, so that all of them shall call on the name of the Lord and serve him with one accord."[15]

If he does not succeed to this extent or is killed, it is certain he is not the one whom the Torah promised. Indeed, he would be like all the perfect and legitimate kings of the house of David who died. The Holy One, blessed be He, would have established his reign only to test the multitude. As it is said: "And some of those who are wise shall stumble, to refine and to purify them and to make them white, until the time of the end; for the appointed time has not yet come."[16]

Daniel long ago prophesied about Jesus of Nazareth, who imagined he was the messiah and was killed by a court of law.[17] As it is said: "And men of violence among your own people shall elevate themselves to establish a vision, but they shall fail."[18] Is there any failure[19] greater than this? All the prophets declared that the messiah will redeem Israel, save them, gather their dispersed, and strengthen their [obedience to] the commandments. But he caused Israel to perish by the sword and to have their remnant scattered and degraded. He replaced the Torah and led astray most of the world to serve a god besides the Lord.

However, man does not have the power to grasp the thoughts of the Creator of the world, for our ways are not His ways and our thoughts are not His thoughts. All those words of Jesus of Nazareth and of this Ishmaelite[20] who arose after him are only to make straight the path for the messianic king and to prepare the whole world to serve the Lord together. As it is said: "For then I will change the speech of the peoples to a pure speech so that all of them shall call on the name of the Lord and serve him with one accord."[21]

How will this take place? The whole world has already been filled with words about the messiah, the Torah, and the commandments. These words have spread to distant islands and among many peoples with uncircumcised hearts. They discuss these words and the commandments of the Torah. Some say these commandments were once true, but now have become void and are not to be followed in all generations. Others say that they contain secret meanings and are not to be understood according to their plain sense, that the messiah has already come and revealed their secrets. [But] when the messianic king truly arises and he has success and is elevated and exalted, all of them will return at once and know that their fathers inherited a lie and that their prophets and their fathers led them astray.

Chapter Twelve

1. Let no one think that the custom of the world will in any way cease to exist during the days of the messiah or that something new will occur in the Work of Creation.[1] No, the world will follow its usual custom. What is said in Isaiah—"And the wolf shall dwell with the lamb, and the leopard shall lie down with the kid"[2]—is a metaphor and a riddle. The meaning is that Israel will live in security with the wicked men of the world,[3] who are compared to a wolf and a leopard. As it is said: "A wolf of the desert shall plunder them, and a leopard stands watch against their cities."[4] All of them will return to the true religion,[5] and will neither rob nor destroy, but will eat what is in abundance at ease with Israel. As it is said: "And the lion shall eat straw like the ox."[6] So too, everything similar to these words on the subject of the messiah is a metaphor. In the days of the messianic king, what the metaphor refers to and what subject is hinted at will become known to everyone.

2. The wise men said: "There is no difference between this world and the days of the messiah, except for [the elimination of] subjugation to the [wicked] kingdoms."[7] It appears from the plain sense of the words of the prophets that at the beginning

of the days of the messiah, the war of Gog and Magog will take place,[8] and that before the war of Gog and Magog, a prophet will arise to set Israel straight and to prepare their hearts. As it is said: "Behold, I will send you Elijah, etc."[9] He does not come to declare that the clean is unclean or the unclean is clean,[10] nor to disqualify people presumed to be of legitimate descent or to make legitimate those who have been disqualified,[11] but [he comes] to establish peace in the world. As it is said: "And he shall turn the heart of the fathers to the children."[12] Some of the wise men say that before the coming of the messiah, Elijah will come. A man does not know how all these things and their like will take place until they do take place, for they remain sealed with the prophets. The wise men, too, have no tradition concerning these things; they can only decide by examining the verses, and they therefore disagree about these matters. In any case, neither the sequence of these events nor the details concerning them are principles[13] of the religion. A man should never occupy himself with the words of *Haggadah*[14] nor spend much time on the *Midrashim*[15] which speak of these matters and the like. Nor should he regard them as having the status of a principle,[16] for they bring about neither fear nor love. Nor should he calculate the end. The wise men said: "May the spirit of those who calculate the end[17] expire."[18] But he shall wait [for the messiah] and believe in the matter in general, as we have explained.

3. In the days of the messianic king, after his dominion is secure and all Israel is gathered unto him, the genealogy of them all will be determined by him by means of the holy spirit that will rest upon him. As it is said: "And he shall sit as a refiner and purifier, etc."[19] First he will purify the descendants of Levi, saying: "This one has the genealogy of a priest, that one the genealogy of a Levite."[20] He will relegate to the [class of] Israelite those who have no such genealogy. For it says: "The governor said to them [that they should not eat the most holy food] until there would be a priest with Urim and Tummim."[21] Thus you learn that it is by means of the holy spirit that the correct genealogies will be ascertained and announced. He will ascertain the genealogy of Israelites only by tribe, announcing that this man is from such-and-such a tribe and another is from such-and-such a tribe. But he does not say

concerning those presumed to be of legitimate descent: "This one is a bastard, that one a slave." For the law is that a family that has become intermingled is [simply] intermingled.

4. The wise men and the prophets longed for the days of the messiah not in order to rule over the whole world, nor to subjugate the nations,[22] nor so that those peoples would be elevated, nor to eat, drink, and be merry, but in order to have leisure for the Torah and its wisdom—with no one to oppress or obstruct them—so that they would merit the life of the world-to-come, as we have explained in *Laws Concerning Repentance*.[23]

At that time, there will not be hunger, or war, or envy and rivalry. For the good things[24] will overflow in great abundance, all the delicacies will be as accessible as the dust of the earth, and the occupation of the whole world will be solely to know the Lord. Therefore Israelites will be great wise men, knowing the concealed[25] things and attaining knowledge of their Creator, depending upon the power of the man. As it is said: "For the earth shall be full of the knowledge of the Lord, as the waters cover the sea."[26]

GUIDE OF THE PERPLEXED

PART III

Chapter 11

These great evils that come about between the human individuals who inflict them upon one another because of purposes, desires, opinions, and beliefs, are all of them likewise consequent upon privation. For all of them derive from ignorance, I mean from a privation of knowledge. Just as a blind man, because of absence of sight, does not cease stumbling, being wounded, and also wounding others, because he has nobody to guide him on his way, the various sects of men—every individual according to the extent of his ignorance—does to himself and to others great evils from which individuals of the species suffer. If there were knowledge, whose relation to the human form is like that of the power of sight to the eye, they would refrain from doing any harm to themselves and to others. For through cognition of the truth, enmity and hatred are removed and the inflicting of harm by people on one another is abolished. It holds out this promise, saying: *And the wolf shall dwell with the lamb, and the leopard shall lie down with the kid, and so on. And the cow and the bear shall feed, and so on. And the sucking child shall play, and so on.*[1] Then it gives the reason for this, saying that the cause of the abolition of these enmities, these discords, and these tyrannies, will be the knowledge that men will then have concerning the true reality of the deity. For it says: *They shall not hurt nor destroy in all My holy mountain; for the earth shall be full of the knowledge of the Lord, as the waters cover the sea.*[2] Know this.

NOTES

PEREQ ḤELEQ

1. I.e., the Israelites.
2. *al-shām*. See W. Bacher, "Schām Als Name Palästina's," *Jewish Quarterly Review*, XVIII (April 1906), pp. 564–65.
3. According to the *Letter to Yemen*, the miracles that will appear through the messiah will astonish the nations to such an extent that they will make peace with him (ed. A. Halkin, Arabic, pp. 90-92, English, p. xvii). However, cf. *M.T.*, Laws of Kings and Their Wars, XI 3, according to which the messiah would not have to perform any miracles.
4. *B.T.*, Sanhedrin, 99a; Berakhot, 34b; Shabbat, 151b; Pesaḥim, 68a.
5. Literally: The powerful and the weak will be in relation to one another. Earlier in *Pereq Ḥeleq* Maimonides refers to people who ask: "When the messiah comes, will he establish equality between the rich and the poor, or will the powerful and the weak be [found] in his days?" (Kafiḥ, p. 197) The answer is given here.
6. *B.T.*, Shabbat, 30b.
7. Isa. 61:5.
8. R. Gamliel, who had said: "In the future, the land of Israel will yield fine bread and woolen garments."
9. Prov. 26:4. R. Gamliel's exchange with the student is cited in the *Talmud* to illustrate the meaning of this verse.
10. Isa. 11:9.
11. Micah 4:3.
12. Isa. 42:4.
13. Ps. 2:7.
14. Or: As it is promised.
15. Jer. 31:34. The complete verse reads: "And a man shall no longer teach his brother or his neighbor, saying, 'Know the Lord,' for they shall all know Me, from the least of them to the greatest, says the Lord; for I will forgive their iniquity, and I will remember their sin no more."
16. Jer. 31:33.

17. Ezek. 36:26.
18. I.e., the anonymous sage who was the source of the Mishnaic passage under discussion.
19. *Mishnah,* Sanhedrin, X 1.
20. Maimonides had explained earlier in *Pereq Heleq* that to serve out of love means to pursue the truth for its own sake alone (Kafih, p. 199).
21. Ps. 32:9.
22. I.e., the prophets and the sages.
23. Hab. 2:3.
24. The text has the plural.
25. *B.T.,* Sanhedrin, 97b. The original passage reads: "May the bones of those who calculate the ends expire."
26. Num. 24:15–19.
27. Deut. 30:3–5. The words, "You stand" (Deut. 29:9), are at the beginning of the section from the Torah containing the verses referred to by Maimonides.

LAWS CONCERNING REPENTANCE

1. Deut. 22:7.
2. Num. 15:31.
3. The italics are not in the text.
4. The text has the plural.
5. Literally: with complete and correct knowledge (*de'ah*).
6. Literally: goodness of soul.
7. The text has the singular.
8. Deut. 6:25.
9. Deut. 32:15.
10. Literally: those who forsake.
11. Deut. 28:48, 47. Maimonides reverses the order of the verses in the Torah.
12. Eccles. 9:10.
13. *Panuy.* This word was translated above in this chapter as leisure (pars. 4 and 6).
14. Isa. 11:9.
15. Jer. 31:34. The complete verse reads: "And a man shall no longer teach his brother or his neighbor, saying: 'Know the Lord,' for they shall all know Me, from the least of them to the greatest, says the Lord; for I will forgive their iniquity, and I will remember their sin no more."
16. Ezek. 36:26.
17. I.e., closer to God than Moses was (*qarov mimosheh*). This reading in the extraordinary Bodleian text of Hyamson's edition agrees with the Rome edition of 1480 and the Constantinople edition of 1509, as well as with some of the manuscripts listed in

Lieberman. The Warsaw-Vilna edition and Hyamson's suggested emendation (based on the traditonal version) read: "approaching Moses" (*qarov lemosheh*). According to the *Letter to Yemen*, although the rank of the messiah will not reach that of Moses, the messiah will be distinguished in certain respects beyond the eminence of Moses (ed. A. Halkin, Arabic, p. 86, English, pp. xvi–xvii). Maimonides lays special emphasis there on Psalm 2:7— "You are My son; this day have I begotten you"—a verse that indicates how close the messiah will be to God. (Cf. *C.M.,* Pereq Ḥeleq *supra,* p. 167). It should not be surprising that in some respects the messiah will be even greater than Moses, because the messiah will have an even greater task: to teach *all* the nations the way of the Lord and to bring peace to the whole world.

18. Isa. 2:2; Micah 4:1.
19. Literally: the first wise men.
20. *B.T.,* Sanhedrin, 99a; Berakhot, 34b; Shabbat, 151b; Pesaḥim, 68a.

LAWS OF KINGS AND THEIR WARS

Chapter Eleven

1. *Mishpatim,* sometimes translated as "judgments."
2. Deut. 30:3, 4, 5. The complete verses read: "And the Lord your God will turn your captivity and have mercy upon you and return and gather you from all the peoples where the Lord your God has scattered you. If your dispersion will reach the extremity of the heavens, from there the Lord your God will gather you and from there He will take you. And the Lord your God will bring you into the land which your fathers possessed and you will possess it; and He will do good to you and make you more numerous than your fathers."
3. Reading with the Rome edition. In place of the words, "from the hand of the sons of Esau," the Venice edition reads: "in the end." The latter words are bracketed in the Warsaw-Vilna edition.
4. Num 24:17. Maimonides interprets each phrase in the verse as referring to one of the two messiahs.
5. II Sam. 8:2.
6. Num. 24:17. According to the *Letter to Yemen,* Num. 24:17 indicates, among other things, that the messiah will exterminate his enemies (ed. A. Halkin; Arabic, p. 78, English, p. xv).
7. Zech. 9:10.
8. Num. 24:18.
9. II Sam. 8:14. The original verse reads: "And all the Edomites became slaves of David."
10. Num 24:18.
11. Obad. 1:21.

12. Deut. 19:8–9. The reference is to three additional cities of refuge, beyond the Jordan River, where someone who has accidentally killed a man could live in safety and not be harmed by a relative of the victim.
13. Ben Koziba, also known as Bar Kokhba, led an unsuccessful revolt in Judea against Rome (132–135 C.E.).
14. Cf. Maimonides' *Letter on Astrology,* where he says that the sin causing the earlier destruction of the Temple was a preoccupation with astrology and the consequent neglect of the art of war (English trans. by R. Lerner, in *Medieval Political Philosophy: A Sourcebook,* ed. by Lerner and Mahdi [New York: Macmillan, 1963], p. 229).
15. Zeph. 3:9.
16. Dan. 11:35.
17. From the beginning of this sentence to the end of the chapter, the translation is based on the Rome edition and the Venice edition.
18. Dan. 11:14.
19. Or: stumbling block.
20. Muhammad.
21. Zeph. 3:9.

Chapter Twelve

1. Literally: Beginning. The expression, "Work (or Account) of the Beginning," is used by Maimonides to refer to natural science.
2. Isa. 11:6.
3. Reading with the Rome edition. The Venice edition reads: "wicked men of the nations." The Warsaw-Vilna edition reads: "wicked men of the idolators."
4. Jer. 5:6.
5. Or: the religion of the truth.
6. Isa. 11:7.
7. *B.T.,* Sanhedrin, 99a; Berakhot, 34b; Shabbat, 151b; Pesaḥim, 68a.
8. Ezek. 38–39.
9. Malachi 3:23.
10. The messiah will not change, for example, the dietary laws.
11. The messiah will not change, for example, the status of a bastard. According to Jewish law, a bastard is the offspring of an adulterous or incestuous union.
12. Malachi 3:24.
13. Literally: root. The text has the singular.
14. The text has the plural: *Haggadot.*
15. The text reads: *Midrashot.*
16. Literally: root.
17. The text has the plural.

18. *B.T.*, Sanhedrin, 97b. The original passage reads: "May the bones of those who calculate the ends expire."
19. Malachi 3:3.
20. The differentiation of the priests and the Levites is a prerequisite for the restoration of the sacrificial cult.
21. Ezra 2:63. The Urim and Tummim were oracular media by means of which a priest predicted a future event.
22. Reading with the Rome edition and the Venice edition. The Warsaw-Vilna edition reads: the idolators.
23. *M.T.*, Laws Concerning Repentance, IX 8.
24. Literally: the good.
25. *Setumim,* translated in XII 2 as "sealed."
26. Isa. 11:9.

GUIDE OF THE PERPLEXED

1. Isa. 11:6–8.
2. Isa. 11:9.